OSCAR MICHEAUX
A Biography

...Dakota Homesteader, Author, Pioneer Film Maker

Betti Carol VanEpps-Taylor

Published by ⊕ Dakota West Books
Dave Strain
P.O. Box 9324
Rapid City, SD 57709

Copy Editor: Norman E. Nelson

Printed in the United States of America by Pine Hill Press, Inc., Sioux Falls, SD 57106.

Library of Congress Cataloging-In-Publication Data:
Library of Congress Catalog Number 98-72905
ISBN Paperback: 1-893250-03-2
        Hard Cover: 1-893250-04-0

Oscar Micheaux: VanEpps-Taylor, Betti Carol
    A Biography of Oscar Micheaux:
    Homesteader, Writer, Film Maker,
    African American
    Includes bibliographical references.
    ISBN
    1. Oscar Micheaux, 1884-1951. 2. Biography 3. African American 4. Film Maker 5. Homesteader 6. Novelist

For Roosevelt and Osie Harris,

with love and gratitude...

ABOUT THE AUTHOR

Betti Carol VanEpps-Taylor is a social historian specializing in African American history of the upper Midwest. She is a native South Dakotan. As a participant-observer of black life on the west coast and in Denver during the turbulent 1950-1970s through marriage to a conservative black activist, she is uniquely qualified to examine the life and work of Oscar Micheaux, especially as he was influenced by life on the unforgiving Great Plains. Ms. VanEpps-Taylor, formerly a senior manager with the U.S. Environmental Protection Agency in Washington, D.C., and Kansas City, Missouri, holds a master's degree in history from the University of South Dakota and has taught history at Wayne State College, Wayne, Nebraska. She currently at work on a new book, *Hiding in Plain Sight: The African American Experience in Dakota Territory and South Dakota, 1802-1970.*

AUTHOR'S PREFACE

This project was originally the subject of a Master's Degree thesis in connection with my studies in upper midwestern history at the University of South Dakota under the direction of Dr. Herbert T. Hoover. During this leisurely three year "third career" program, I was fortunate to have the ongoing encouragement, advice, and peer review of several outstanding scholars in residence who helped me combine my interest in African American history with my love for the upper midwest heartland and its unique historical role. Indeed, I was honored when the USD History Department selected the thesis as its nominee for the 1999 Distinguished Master's Thesis Award sponsored by the Midwestern Association of Graduate Schools.

Many people helped me with this biography. The members of South Dakota's Gregory County Oscar Micheaux Society promoted the state's belated recognition of Oscar Micheaux as homesteader and influential filmmaker. Their annual, nationally publicized Oscar Micheaux Film Festival, begun in 1996, has created a forum for local and national Micheaux scholars. In turn, the encouragement of the local history buffs, especially Lee Arlie Barry, Richard Papousek, Francie Johnson, and Ted Blakey, and national humanities scholars, Pearl Bowser, Ron Green, Janis Hebert Hausman, Learthen Dorsey, and Charlene Regester has been gratifying. I extend a personal thanks to Harley W. Robinson, Jr., for his special willingness to share his family knowledge and personal recollections of Oscar Micheaux.

Dr. Kurt Hackemer helped update my African American historiography and worked with me on a program that introduced Oscar Micheaux's films to the USD student body. Dr. Thomas J. Gasque provided the perspective of scholars of English and literary criticism on Micheaux's writings. Dr. Hoover's unfailing generosity with his time, patience, and general mentoring was a source of continual inspiration and sustenance. Outstanding cooperation from the inter-library loan service at I.D. Weeks

Library, University of South Dakota, and the South Dakota State Historical Society made it possible for me to gain access to materials not otherwise available locally. Norman E. Nelson earned my profound gratitude for patiently steering me through the intricacies of copy editing. The staff at Pine Hill Press provided invaluable assistance and counsel in creating a well-designed and well-presented volume. I am especially indebted to my South Dakota publisher, David Strain, of Dakota West Books, for his enthusiastic support in every aspect of bringing this effort to publication and placing it before Micheaux fans and scholars throughout the country. It was David who urged me to explore and expand my understanding of the homestead period in Micheaux's life — a contribution to Micheaux lore that can best be made by one with roots in the prairie. In the essence of the homesteading experience lies the seeds of the man Oscar Micheaux was to become; and because of it, his life and work remind us all that we are more alike than we are different.

On a personal note, my gratitude is extended to several very important individuals. First, I am grateful to Dr. Richard Peters of Washington, D.C., whose timely intervention effectively removed me from the "Washington Merry-Go-Round" and gave me back my life. Next, I appreciate my husband, Joseph Brown Bear Taylor, for his support and understanding during this lengthy writing process, support that frequently involved his assuming "house husband" duties to allow me to write. I would like to thank my granddaughters, Korey and Katie Graham: Korey for her steadfast encouragement and unwavering belief that her grandmother "can be anything", and Katie for her cheerful help with the editing process through several versions of both thesis and book manuscripts. My ninety year old mother, Martha Grow VanEpps, faithfully read too many drafts and was willing to engage in a belated enjoyment of Oscar Micheaux's early books. Finally, I would like to thank my good friend, Nap Harris, Director of Student Life at California State University, Long Beach, California, for his support and encouragement and for more than 40 years of continuing reality check on Black America.

Betti Carol VanEpps-Taylor
Buhl, Idaho, 1999

FOREWORD

BY HERBERT T. HOOVER, PH.D.

Perhaps no one is adequately qualified to introduce a biography of Oscar Micheaux because his life gave expression to so many themes in national history. Approximately a generation after the liberation of slaves in the United States, he was born into an African American family in a community close to the former Mason-Dixon line, where elders encouraged younger members to seek opportunities elsewhere. Quickly, Micheaux followed other black people into occupations where they could gain self reliance and personal freedom.

His first place of relocation was Chicago, where at the time, dozens of ethnic groups assembled because of job opportunities in manufacturing and commercial industries. In the windy city, like the Polish, Irish, Hungarian, Hispanic, or other immigrant, he could find employment suited to his own background and skills. A rapid gathering of African Americans supplied a modicum of ethnic security.

On the railroad, as a porter, Micheaux played a deferential role in an occupation that attracted African American men. As a job, this not only provided a fairly respectable income, but also gave access to information about the methods of entrepreneurship utilized by the travelers he served. Like many other black men, he rode the rails only as long as necessary to find his way into a more suitable occupation.

The lure of the West, so heavily publicized by Horace Greeley, was in his mind when he decided to relocate beyond the Mississippi River. Beyond his own writings, no evidence survives to indicate why he decided to challenge a hostile natural environment on the northern Great Plains. Nor do his collections leave a clue to why he did not follow courses of action taken by other African Americans who settled here. Oscar Micheaux must have known that beyond Sioux City, Iowa, the town with the largest black enclave was Yankton, South Dakota, where African Americans long had been residents because of a demand for their services in the Missouri River steamboat industry. He must have heard that some black porters left their trains to settle and marry into Native American societies — for example, at the Devil's Lake, North Dakota, and Fort Peck, North Dakota, reservations. He might have known that, similarly, some had abandoned their steamboat jobs to marry into tribes at South Dakota's Yankton and Lower Brule reservations. Some had assembled with other African Americans in an agricultural enclave north of Pierre known as the Sully Colony. For a reason he never revealed, Micheaux avoided all other African Americans and chose to join settlements that evolved at the east end of the Rosebud Reservation.

He might not have known that he was selecting the most international of all Sioux reservation societies, that for more than two generations had engaged in direct exposure to outsiders along the Missouri River—including many blacks who served at nearby Fort Randall. In any event, he struck out on his own to join a pool of Caucasian settlers who took advantage of successive reductions in the boundaries of the Rosebud Reservation to settle in adjacent counties.

Like many who occupied farmsteads on the northern Great Plains, evidently Oscar Micheaux never intended to stay but only to earn a nest egg. Soon he sold or lost his land through foreclosure during those last hard years, and launched a career as a writer of fiction whose themes closely resembled developments in his own life. At Sioux City, he learned to publish and market his literature. From the publication of books he moved into a pioneering role as the producer of movies that featured not only African American cultural circumstances but also black actors.

To the end of his life, Oscar Micheaux endured the burden of indebtedness from the production of movies and the sting of negative treatment by both literary and movie critics. In the wake of the Civil Rights Movement, however, critics revisited his work and began to view him as an ethnic pioneer.

Through every phase of his adult life, Oscar Micheaux earned his belated recognition as a legitimate celebrity. Any reader with interests in the movement of African Americans to cities near the onset of the twentieth century, the participation of black people in agricultural settlement on the northern Great Plains, early manifestations of ethnic literature and, most of all, the pioneering production of movies by, about, and for black people will enjoy this volume. Written in a delightful narrative style by an author with a protracted personal experience as the mother of an African American family, this — the first biography of Oscar Micheaux to appear in book form — will find a permanent place in national ethnic literature.

Herbert T. Hoover
University of South Dakota.

TABLE OF CONTENTS

LIST OF ILLUSTRATIONS

(Following page 91)

South Dakota Map

1911 Winner Street Scene

1907 Gregory Street Scene

"First Day's Filing" - Tripp County

Historical Marker at First Homestead

Replica of Oscar Micheaux's
First Homestead

Movie Poster: *The Exile* (1931)

Movie Poster: *Swing* (1938)

Grave of Oscar Micheaux,
Great Bend, Kansas

CHAPTER 1
SETTING THE STAGE

Oscar Micheaux (1884-1951), black film maker, novelist, and South Dakota homesteader, languished in obscurity for many years until a renewed interest in silent film preservation brought his work to life for a new audience of film enthusiasts scattered throughout the world and representing a wide variety of cultures. Interest in Micheaux's films has sparked a companion interest in his seven novels. Two of them, *The Conquest: The Story of a Negro Pioneer*, and *The Homesteader*, recently have been reprinted in belated recognition of their value as accurate accounts of homesteading, town building, and railroading on the Upper Great Plains. *The Homesteader* became Micheaux's first film, an epic that exposed African Americans of his era to the unfamiliar and romantic wilds of the northern prairie.

The other novels, long considered by critics to be less important to the overall body of his work, may also see a renaissance. Not only do they carry strong and consistent autobiographical overtones that provide tantalizing clues to the persona of this intensely private man, they also provide significant insights into aspects of American life, black and white, over a period of some 30 definitive years.[1]

Ironically, the rediscovery of Micheaux's books and films by African American film scholars has coincided with a search for their homesteading heritage by the mostly-white northern plains settlers' great-grandchildren. Both are topics largely ignored by mainstream historians and 20th century popular culture. The result of this juxtaposition has been a unique opportunity for cross-cultural understanding. The film scholars have turned to

Micheaux's prairie novels and the homesteaders' great-grandchildren to understand his work, and the homesteaders' descendants have turned to the black scholars and the writings of this lone black pioneer to understand their ancestors' daily struggle to build new lives in a harsh land.

Enthusiasts and critics, especially academicians, will continue to debate whether to include Micheaux in an elite group remembered as "Black Renaissance" writers and artists. Such an exercise is as futile as a debate regarding whether to classify Herman Melville as a "Romanticist" or a thoughtful observer of America's brief venture into imperialism, when he wrote his epic of high adventure and social commentary, *Moby Dick*. If Micheaux is excluded from Black Renaissance performers and artists, should Louis Armstrong, Cab Calloway, and even Duke Ellington also be excluded? Anyway, it is a moot point. Oscar Micheaux must be included in an ethnic renaissance that exploded during the 1920s.

While most current research about Micheaux takes place among a growing coterie of scholars that concentrates on the rescue of early black-cast films, my interest in this conservative African American entrepreneur derives from my immersion in black life as a result of an early inter-racial marriage. From 1956 to 1969 I was a member by marriage of an African American family whose values mirrored many of those expressed by Oscar Micheaux in *The Conquest*. Subsequently, as the single parent of a mixed-race daughter, I experienced, and continue to observe, the many changes that have engulfed black America. And, as a native South Dakotan descended from the homesteaders, I have a keen interest in those hardy, largely forgotten African Americans who chose, however briefly, to make the windswept prairies their home. I have long believed that the climate and isolation of the Upper Midwest leave an indelible mark on its people, and I remain intrigued by Micheaux's response to the land and curious about how it affected his life, work, and philosophy.

Other black film makers were already experimenting with the medium when the self-taught Micheaux burst on the scene, but he was the first successfully to complete and market a full length, eight-reel, black-cast motion picture, *The Homesteader*. During his 30-year career he made and marketed more than 40 films (the actual number is in dispute). They appeared nearly every year from 1919 to 1941. After an eight year hiatus to return to writing, he made his last film in 1949. That film, *The Betrayal*, presented his late-life novel, *The Wind From Nowhere*, a story that returned to his South Dakota homesteading roots.

Always operating on a shoestring budget, he wrote many of his own scripts, creating exciting, fast-moving stories with wide appeal among diverse African American audiences. Many of his films, while designed to entertain, used the medium as a "bully pulpit" from which he proclaimed his message of personal improvement, independence, and initiative, while educating his viewers about the "Great Northwest" with its unlimited opportunity.

Like other early films, most of Micheaux's have disappeared. The few rediscovered titles surfaced at odd places around the world, often with foreign language sub-titles. Preserved, translated back into English, and studied, they provide both entertainment and endless opportunities for speculation and conjecture about the man, his output, and the way he viewed his world. Often his work was controversial when it appeared, and it remains so today, although for different reasons that pertain to changing political and social values.

Micheaux's outlook reflected the chaotic philosophical divisions in African American communities in the early twentieth century. Some four million former slaves and their more experienced, previously freed brethren struggled in diverse and often contradictory ways to unite, create communities, and reach for the American dream. As an idealistic, independent loner who, in his early years, traveled widely throughout the United States, Micheaux developed an outlook that reflected his perceptions of those variations, which represented sectionalism, class differences, and conflict between city and farm.

Coming of age in the virulent white racism of the late nineteenth and early twentieth centuries, he had been exposed to both the racist pseudo-science and the imperialist, jingoist politics that pervaded the national mentality — black as well as white. During his era also, many people still believed in the Horatio Alger mythology wherein an ambitious, competent, hard working, and lucky individual could achieve breathtaking material success. Many believed that the best place to try one's luck was on the "last frontier" of the west.

Within black America, new leadership challenged the prevailing wisdom of Booker T. Washington's accommodationist views with the scholarly, militantly assertive views expressed by Harvard-educated sociologist W.E.B. DuBois. At the opposite intellectual and social scale, disillusioned separatists participated in Marcus Garvey's chaotic "Back to Africa" movement. Between these extreme positions, a silent majority struggled to survive in an increasingly racist society and to raise their families in personalized versions of the American dream. Others, to the embarrassment of aspirants, survived as a stereotypical underclass in colorful and bitter hand-to-mouth urban and rural poverty.

Well into the twentieth century, the simply-stated ideas of Booker T. Washington permeated black society through black newspapers and pulpits long before mainstream whites became aware of them. Washington's ideas of self-help, ambition, and personal achievement continued to resonate with a largely silent but significant group of conservative, often rural, upwardly mobile, black families. They remained aloof from the philosophical debate raging among the factions and raised their children in Washingtonian values, similar to those of aspiring European immigrants and other white families. Such was the nature of the Michaux (original spelling) family.

Born in 1884 and attaining adolescence during the height of Washington's popularity, Oscar Micheaux was an early and ardent follower of the Alabama educator's principles of entrepreneurship, ambition, and self-help, but he could not accept Washington's belief that the South offered black Americans their best hope. Over the years, Micheaux's political and social beliefs steadily changed as he matured as a filmmaker and writer, although he continued to believe that African Americans' best hope lay in an expanded middle class. That middle class, he believed, could best prosper if individuals would establish businesses or seize the unlimited opportunities for successful farming ventures in the "Great Northwest".

The emerging post-Reconstruction black middle class was tiny, consisting of Negroes freed before the Civil War and postwar freedmen who were either extraordinarily well equipped or lucky. These middle-class African Americans found careers as educators, artisans, shopkeepers, and service workers. A few knowledgeable farmers were fortunate enough to own land. Together, they constituted a rising group that soon included a small contingent of business owners and a larger number of college professors and preachers who assumed positions of racial leadership. According to black sociologist E. Franklin Frazier, these individuals accounted for less than five per cent of the total black population, leaving the vast majority in a struggle for places on the bottom rungs of the social ladder.[2]

Daily, that struggling majority faced daunting pressure and suggestions for success from pulpit and newspaper editors as middle-class leaders attempted to motivate African Americans to raise their sights, achieve educational credentials, and "become a credit to the race". The black church and black popular culture reflected these pressures, which included strong community disapproval of marrying or "consorting" outside the race and were soon to include undertones of color prejudice that discriminated against those of darker complexion.

In his autobiographical novel, *The Conquest*, Micheaux describes how he came to believe that he would find his destiny as a racial role model whose life would demonstrate a realistic path to success that others might follow. Over his lifetime he found a place not only as role model, but also as myth maker and social critic. As the author of books and creator of films for and about African Americans, his work reached audiences across the entire spectrum of black life. Some of his caustic criticisms and satirical social commentaries offended or evoked misunderstanding by audiences or critics. Because he was a self-taught writer and film maker without credentials from one of the black colleges, African American critics who were stung by the truths inherent in his works resorted to technical criticism. Over the years, critiques ran a gamut from accommodationist to racist. Some criticism was more indicative of the critics' personal biases than realistic perceptions about the cultural circumstances Micheaux's work examined.

A complex and contradictory personality, he remains difficult to understand. He believed absolutely that "a colored man" could be anything he desired if he were willing to work for it.[3] Moreover, he thought that if he could accomplish great things, so could anyone else who was willing to make a similar commitment. He had little patience with members of his race whom he perceived as unwilling or unable to make the effort. Indeed, each of his books and many of his films featured "colored men" in professional roles or prestigious circumstances that might have been considered highly unusual for the times. For example, in his second book, *The Forged Note*, the protagonist is a former South Dakota writer-homesteader turned entrepreneur who is developing a successful system for marketing his books throughout the South. In one of his early films, *The Gunsaulis Mystery*, a black lawyer represents a Jewish businessman accused of murdering a young white girl. In *Within Our Gates*, his second film, one finds an African American mining engineer as well as the more typical minister-educator operating a school in the South for black children.

In his paired detective stories, written late in life, the reader finds a skilled and highly trusted black detective who specializes in insurance fraud cases, several wealthy, land-owning African American physicians, a highly-educated mixed-race spy for the Nazis, and a successful motion picture magnate. In each of the homestead novels, as well as in the several films dealing with frontier material, African American men appear as wealthy and respected farmers, ranchers, or frontiersmen, or as successful land speculators who have made their version of the Horatio Alger tale come true. His portrayals of women, too, reflected his belief that any job open to a white woman in that admittedly restrictive period, could as well be done by a woman of color.

At a time when black entrepreneurs faced hardship and suffered high rates of failure, Micheaux wrote, published, and sold his novels and successfully produced and marketed his films. Yet they never earned reviews by the literati of the Harlem Renaissance who were actively encouraging other black writers and artists, and were largely ignored as flimsy examples of popular culture. Perhaps the frontier world portrayed in *The Conquest* and *The Homesteader* seemed irrelevant in the face of widespread urban migration and the explosion of urban black culture that characterized Harlem. His later novels likewise appear to have been mostly ignored by the black media, although they were sustained by a core of faithful readers. Journalist Richard Gehr avers that Micheaux's mystery, *The Case of Mrs. Wingate*, sold in excess of 50,000 copies in the early 1940's, and *The Wind From Nowhere* appeared in at least nine editions.[4]

In any case, Oscar Micheaux — the man, the writer and the filmmaker — remains an enigma. Clues to his life and thoughts emerge only in scattered facts and in the body of his works. He has been called arrogant, puritanical, ignorant, stubborn, penny pinching, atheistic, egotistical, racist, and a charlatan. He might have been all of these, but he was also charming, pragmatic, bold, self-confident, assertive, independent, and mainly successful. Although he considered himself a "great Race Man" who always supported the "uplift of Negroes", critics vilified him for the views he expressed in literature as well as in films.

Then and now, he drew criticism for calling attention to embarrassing flaws within black society, flaws typical of any large and diverse group emerging from oppression, and for examining and perhaps supporting the color, ethnic, and class prejudices present in African American circles. Micheaux believed that his films and books portrayed an accurate cross-section of black America with both positive and negative dimensions, and that this broad portrayal was central and essential to the integrity of his work. One black film scholar remarked that watching an old Micheaux film was like catching members of one's family in public without clothes.[5]

Surely, Micheaux knew that these negative portrayals would be a source of embarrassment within black communities and that they might even fuel the racism rampant in the white world. Yet it appears that he considered the presentation of these "honest views" vital to his personal and professional integrity regardless of the cost. Though it might be of small consolation to sensitive

African Americans, careful readers of Oscar Micheaux's books will find that he scrutinized nearly everyone he encountered with the same jaundiced, irreverent, critical, and sometimes biased eye, caricaturing and commenting freely on personal qualities, foibles, follies, and prejudices of Jews, Irishmen, Native Americans, and plain vanilla white people with equal enthusiasm.

In recent years, black and white scholars alike have attempted to shed light on this complex man, who chose never directly to expose his private life. To date, no scholar has examined Micheaux's persona against the backdrop of family that bred and nurtured him, early years in Illinois, maturation while at work on the railroad, and success as a homesteader on the Great Plains. All of these experiences enabled him to place American blacks in a unique context. One key to Micheaux's social views and philosophy and to the man himself lies in the context of his background, much of which we can only surmise from his fictionalized autobiography and novels and the few contemporary primary sources extant.

As a young man, Oscar Micheaux successfully bridged many worlds: black and white, urban and rural, upper and lower class, remote, cold northern prairie environment and warm, populous southern society. In bridging these worlds, often as a participant and always as an observer, Micheaux gained an understanding and developed a viewpoint that significantly influenced his personal philosophy and became a part of his books and films. Indeed, his novels reflected an emerging point of view developed in the context of his own life experiences.

The first of these novels came into print anonymously in 1913. He wrote *The Conquest: The Story of a Negro Pioneer* to raise money after a disastrous marriage, drought, and over-speculation in land created desperate financial conditions. Like other optimistic South Dakota homesteaders who had prospered in years of plentiful rainfall and bumper crops, Micheaux became a casualty of the widespread drought that devastated Great Plains crops in the mid teens and reduced many farmers to foreclosure.

The book appeared as a novel but it did not contain features essential to that genre, and as a consequence evoked sharp criticism. Initially, it found its place instead as an autobiographical memoir, even though he disguised himself and his environment with clever, often rhyming pseudonyms. Evidently he did this to avoid the threat of litigation for slander. Aggressive attorneys, especially in frontier towns during that period, made money by initiating such suits against authors and filmmakers.[6] Recently the book has re-emerged as a homesteading classic; one of the best and most accurate accounts of the practicalities and politics of homesteading, town building, and railroading ever written.

Although Micheaux exercised artistic license, scholars and family members accepted his earliest effort and, indeed, aspects of his later novels, as fairly accurate autobiography.[7] *The Conquest* was his first book, written to express personal anguish, and perhaps to serve as a catharsis. Content that remained personally disturbing and challenging appeared repeatedly in the novels and films and presented alternative endings to the humiliating circumstances that surrounded the failure of his first marriage and his reaction to drought and foreclosure. By contriving fantasy solutions, he might have found a release from the pain and the courage to pursue artistic work. Through subsequent books and films, Micheaux provided insights into his business practices and supplied impressions of urban black cultural centers and their diverse occupants at different historical periods.

The Conquest evoked special interest among South Dakota scholars who recognized the loosely-disguised place names and translated them into a remarkably accurate profile of the opening of the Rosebud country of south central South Dakota. At least one South Dakota high school has used the book to teach local history while correctly identifying Micheaux's fictionalized place names. Knowledgeable Gregory County residents agree that the account is essentially accurate and have successfully verified developments portrayed in *The Conquest* as biographical expressions of Micheaux's personal experiences during his nine years of residence in the area.[8]

For all observers, *The Conquest* serves as the best source regarding the early life of the man. Other information comes from his subsequent novels and from scattered contemporary documents or publications. Many of these are currently under exami-

nation by a wide range of film scholars and historians with vary-
ing agendas, and their perceptions have enriched this study. All
of these, as well as studies of black life in America during this
period and my personal experience, have provided ample
sources for study and speculation about this complex man.

CHAPTER 2
EARLY YEARS

According to his fictionalized autobiography, Oscar Devereaux (Micheaux's pseudonym in *The Conquest: The Story of a Negro Pioneer*) was born near Murphysboro, Illinois, where his father owned an 80-acre farm and earned a reputation for being "well-to-do, that is, for a colored man". He was the fifth child in a family of 13, born on January 2, 1884. Although the "-aux" ending on the family name implied a Louisiana French background, Micheaux stated in *The Conquest* that his father and grandfather came from Kentucky, where his grandfather had been a slave. The Kentucky background suggests a connection to French Huguenot slave owners. Subsequent brief biographies identify Oscar Micheaux's parents as Calvin S. and Belle (Willingham) Michaux and state that Oscar later added the "e" to the original spelling of his surname.[9]

Comparing his description of the geography of his birthplace with maps of the period raises questions about the exact location of the family farm near Murphysboro. The town was a short distance west of Carbondale in Jackson County in the southern third of Illinois known as "Egypt", perhaps because the largest town was Cairo. In antebellum days and immediately after the Civil War, "Egypt" was a term of derision that maligned the lifestyle of white inhabitants as "perverse and crooked, Negrophobic, lazy, ignorant, anti-intellectual, drunkards and slave catchers who held the law in small regard and loved a good fight".[10]

Between 1867 and 1875, the Ku Klux Klan freely operated in the area. Its members, covered by sheets, terrorized blacks as well as poor whites who stepped out of line. As post-war economic growth brought industry to Cairo and the surrounding

area, however, and as the Illinois Central and the Mississippi and
Ohio railroads crossed the region, white homogeneity dissolved
into a racial mixture. Two camps for liberated Negroes appeared:
one near Cairo, the other just north in Saline County. Many black
people settled in the area to escape the prospect of indefinitely
sharecropping for their former southern masters.[11]

During this period, officials in Illinois abolished restrictive
Black Codes, gave African Americans the franchise, and decreed
that education should be integrated.[12] Increasing numbers of liberated blacks flocked to the area because of the legal changes,
and also because the climate and terrain matched agricultural
conditions they had left behind. In the river towns they found
jobs in lumber industries, river commerce, railroad construction,
and transportation.

Most immigrant black families came from Tennessee,
Kentucky, Virginia, Mississippi, Missouri, and Arkansas. They settled along the Ohio River or on the prairie and rolling hills north
from Cairo to Murphysboro and Carbondale and east as far as
Pulaski and Massac counties. By the end of the 19th century they
formed both burgeoning rural settlements and small-town communities.[13]

Apparently, at the time of initial settlement there was little
segregation, although families tended to cluster in kinship or
friendship groups. Black people tried to purchase land wherever
and whenever they could afford it. In pulpits and newspapers,
African American leaders touted the ownership of land in family
farms as the best way for the "colored race" to get ahead. This
message implied cultural as well as socio-economic integration.
By 1900, African Americans in Pulaski County comprised about
40 per cent of the total population and controlled a significant
bloc of votes.[14] Shirley Carlson wrote that:

> ...black status was further strengthened by
> improving political conditions. For example, John J.
> Bird, a Cairo black, was appointed trustee of the
> Illinois Industrial University at Champaign. Black
> newspapers periodically reported the election of
> blacks to public office in southern Illinois. In the

1880s and 1890s area blacks held such positions as county and city councilman, city attorney, county coroner, and police magistrate. In 1892, the *State Capital* argued that Cairo blacks had "fared better than their brothers in any other portion of Illinois".[15]

The Middlewestern black press included the *Cairo Gazette*, a weekly publication that carried news to southern Illinois blacks. Editors of several weekly journals published in Chicago and Springfield and sympathetic white journalists served as agents of social change, carrying information about business enterprise, artistic expression, racial solidarity, and black self-esteem. Newspapers controlled by blacks contained editorial pages that often addressed race matters, classified advertisements, and weekly features that included news from small outlying communities. Mainly, their publishers and editors were educated people: ministers, politicians, schoolteachers, morticians, or Pullman porters. Many were Republicans who strongly promoted partisan values and encouraged citizen participation in public life. Generally, outside the South editors could speak freely without fear of retribution. They produced steady barrages of counsel for hard work, family values, thrift, personal ambition, home ownership, and entrepreneurship — all of the values espoused and publicized by Booker T. Washington.[16]

Although readers must have been receptive, they still lived in an era of transition and uncertainty during which new racial roles and social structures were evolving. As in the Old South, African Americans endured the hardships of farming and indebtedness. Only a few of the "best and brightest" achieved economic stability.[17] Jim Crowism increasingly stifled freedom. Blatant racism that sometimes descended to violence remained alive in Egypt to undermine black solidarity.

Oscar Micheaux was born into this ambiguous social climate where bigoted whites threatened repression alongside black examples of political prominence and material success, and ordinary black folk persisted in their efforts to achieve economic stability and social acceptance. While many in his community were interested only in respite from oppression and an opportunity to enjoy the present without worrying about the future, in young Oscar these conflicting messages aroused an adolescent rebellion. In *The Conquest* and other books, he writes of his frustration with people who seemed so set in their subservient ways that it was hopeless to try to talk them into bettering themselves. Like other African Americans consumed with ambition and hope, he never could understand or accept these attitudes.

Although slavery had denied them the benefits of a formal education, Calvin and Belle Michaux believed strongly in its value for their children. Despite financial hardship, they resolved to relocate in a town where black children could find better educational facilities. Micheaux describes Metropolis, their destination on the Ohio River some 60 miles southeast, as "an old town with a few factories, two flour mills, two or three sawmills, box factories, and another concern where veneering was peeled from wood blocks softened with steam".[18] Here he attended an established, if decrepit, school where he learned his lessons readily and drew criticism for talking too much and asking too many questions. His wry commentary on this experience indicates that he never allowed community disapproval to affect him overmuch:

> This didn't have the effect of burdening me with many friends in M—pls and I was regarded by many of the boys and girls, who led in the whirlpool of the local colored society, as being of the "too-slow-to-catch-cold" variety, and by some of the Elders as being worldly, a free-thinker, and a dangerous associate for young Christian folks.[19]

In an intriguing but uncited article entitled "One Man Show", journalist Richard Gehr wrote that Oscar's individualism, freely delivered opinions, and plethora of private projects prompted his school friends to bestow upon him the nickname of "Oddball".[20]

In *The Conquest*, Micheaux describes the school and some of his siblings:

The local colored school was held in an old building made of plain boards standing straight up and down with batten on the cracks. It was inadequate in many respects; the teachers very often inefficient, and besides, it was far from home. After my oldest sister graduated, she went away to teach [in Carbondale] and about the same time, my oldest brother quit school and went to a nearby town and became a table waiter, much to the dissatisfaction of my mother who always declared emphatically that she wanted none of her sons to become lackeys. When the Spanish-American War broke out, the two brothers above me enlisted with a company of other patriotic young fellows and were taken to Springfield to go into camp. At Springfield their company was disbanded and those of the company that wished to go on were accepted into other companies and those that desired to go home were permitted to do so. The younger of the two brothers returned home by freight; the other joined a Chicago company and was sent to Santiago and later to San Luis DeCuba where he died with typhoid pneumonia.[21]

When circumstances, possibly financial, caused the Michaux family to return to the farm, Oscar grew more unhappy and rebellious, creating problems within the family.

...my father complained of my poor service in the field and in disgust I was sent off to do the marketing—which pleased me for it was not only easy, but gave me the chance to meet and talk with many people—and I always sold the goods and engaged more for the afternoon delivery. I could always do better business for myself than for anyone else. I was not given much credit for my ability to sell, however, until my brother, who complained... was sent to do the marketing. He was not a salesman and lacked the aggressiveness to approach people with a basket, and never talked much; was timid and when spoken to or approached plainly showed it.

...I met and became acquainted with people quite readily. I soon noticed that many people enjoyed being flattered, and how pleased even the prosperous men's wives would seem if I bowed to them with a pleasant, "Good Morning, Mrs. Quante, nice morning and would you care to look at some fresh roasting ears—ten cents a dozen; or some nice ripe strawberries, two boxes for fifteen cents?" "Yes, Maam, Thank You! and O, Mrs. Quante would you care for some radishes, cucumbers or lettuce for tomorrow? I could deliver late this afternoon, you see, for maybe you haven't the time to come to market every day."

From this association I soon learned to try to give each and every customer a different greeting or suggestion, which usually brought a smile and a nod of appreciation as well as a purchase.[22]

Still, the provincialism among local residents annoyed him. In *The Conquest*, Oscar expressed frustration with lifestyles that revolved around church, camp meetings, and saloons. Idealistic and something of a prig, he disapproved of the hypocrisy in the church and clergy which, he claimed, tolerated all manner of un-Christian activity during the week as long as the members showed up on Sunday.

In his subsequent creative work, Micheaux often used personal experience as a medium for the expression of resentment toward parts his life that left permanent scars. His semi-autobiographical third book, *The Homesteader*, included his delight in life on a prairie homestead as well as his anger at the hypocritical preachers of the black church, epitomized for him by his despised father-in-law. The book embodied all of Micheaux's disgust with the black church in general, and its clergy in particular.

In it, he amplifies his previous brief statement in *The Conquest* that his future father-in-law had briefly pastored the family's Metropolis African Methodist Church before being elevated to the position of presiding elder for the Southern District of Illinois. Even then the preacher's reputation for womanizing was well recognized.[23]

The Homesteader account is graphic and disturbing. In the voice of his protagonist, Jean Baptiste, Micheaux writes of being unfairly and brutally whipped by an embarrassed, over-reacting mother at the behest of that visiting clergyman. The adults had been at dinner, where the clergyman was attempting the seduction of a pretty and unwilling guest, only to be interrupted by the repeated intrusions of the seven year old boy who demanded her attention, thwarting the seducer's dishonorable intentions. The resulting punishment was so severe and seemed so unfair that the child ran away, became lost in the woods, and was nearly killed by a catamount.[24]

Although it is not possible to verify the accuracy of these excerpts from disguised and perhaps heavily fictionalized autobiographies, there might be sufficient truth in the tale, when added to the facts of his destroyed marriage, to begin to answer questions about his future portrayals of the church and its clergy.

By the time he was 16, even the extra money he brought home from the farmers' market was not enough to solve the family's financial problems. Swamped with debt, Oscar's father was momentarily rescued by a small inheritance that provided relief and created the opportunity to consider relocation further west. Calvin Michaux's mother, Melvina M. Michaux, and his brother, William, had settled and prospered near Great Bend, Kansas, in the late eighties.[25] Many observers believed the opportunities for African Americans were better and there was less racial tension in Kansas. In *The Homesteader*, Micheaux emphasizes this belief and refers to his uncles who successfully farmed there, contrasting their success with his own over-confidence that led to financial ruin as a South Dakota homesteader.[26]

While the senior Michauxs considered their options, Oscar remained restless, arrogant, and outspoken, alienating peers and elders alike with "persistent declarations that there were not

enough competent colored people to grasp the many opportunities that presented themselves, and that if white people could
possess such nice homes, wealth and luxuries, so in time, could
the colored people".[27] His outbursts engendered stern lectures
from his elders. These adults, reflecting the bitterness of the
times, graphically described the recent anguish of slavery, mount-
ing white prejudice, and hatred for blacks, all conspiring to keep
the black man down. Realizing that he could change no minds,
and with no interest in accompanying his parents on their eventual migration to Kansas, he vowed, in 1901, to prove all of them
wrong by leaving.[28] Locals probably bade him "good riddance"
with their goodbyes.

Oscar's parents and younger siblings did not relocate to
Kansas until 1904. By then, Oscar was experimenting with his
own homestead venture. The parents would prosper in Kansas,
where, according to Micheaux's second cousin, Harley W.
Robinson, Jr., the children still in the home did well. Although
Oscar's grandmother and a younger sister, Olivia, would later join
him briefly in his Rosebud adventure, the other youngsters took
full advantage of opportunities offered around Great Bend and
used the Kansas university system as springboards to professional careers for themselves and their descendants.[29]

Meantime, 16 year old Oscar, with his Horatio Alger complex
intact, was learning that independence and economic success
were elusive. In *The Conquest*, he described his discouraging
efforts to secure sufficient capital. His first jobs were in small
southern Illinois towns where industries hired common labor.
Time in a "car manufacturing plant", [perhaps railroad cars] at
$1.25 a day netted some small savings, as did a job boiling water
in a coal mine at $2.25 a day. Moving on to Carbondale where
his older sister was teaching, he found work and met Jessie, a
lovely but immature high school girl with whom he carried on a
long, half-hearted courtship-by-mail, considering her at one point
as a prospective wife.[30]

Finally he felt mature enough to enter the Chicago area,
where his oldest brother worked as a waiter. On arrival, Oscar
was disgusted to find that his brother's glowing accounts of a
prosperous life had been greatly exaggerated. W.O. Michaux

enjoyed the bright lights and moved from job to job, spending his money on fancy clothing and jewelry while apparently being "kept" by a widow. Although W.O. personally felt no urgency about saving money for the future, he considered it his responsibility to keep an eye on his kid brother, albeit from a safe distance, and sent regular worrisome reports to Oscar's parents charging him

> with the crime of being a big, awkward, ignorant kid, unsophisticated in the ways of the world, and especially of the city; that I was likely to end my "career" by running over a street car [sic] and permitting the city to irretrievably lose me [sic], or something equally bad. When I heard from my mother, she was worried and begged me to come home....

Instead, Oscar rented a place of his own and went to work in the stockyards.[31]

By the year 1901, southern blacks, responding to increasingly intolerable economic and social conditions, had begun a mass migration to northern urban areas. Partly driven by an aggressive advertising campaign mounted by Robert Abbott, publisher of the widely circulated *Chicago Defender*, which began its publication in 1905, Chicago became the destination of choice for many African Americans. As a result, Chicago's black population grew by 148 per cent between 1910 and 1920.[32] A burgeoning economy offered jobs to African Americans in packing houses, warehouses, and coal companies as well as in domestic service. In turn, access to jobs and reasonable wages offered a sense of adventure and a chance to mingle with strangers in communities being fashioned into a cultural center. A newcomer could choose points of access, ranging from the gutter to the church.

Big city life proved as disillusioning to Oscar as life in rural southern Illinois. Stockyard work was hard and unpleasant and the wages were poor. Soon he gave it up and tried the steel mills in nearby Joliet with the same result. After he returned to Chicago, an employment agency swindled him out of two dollars and evoked his determination to become his own boss. Perhaps he could open a shoeshine stand. It required personal initiative but only minimum initial investment and could provide better access to success.

To avoid downtown competition, Micheaux set up his stand at a white suburban barbershop in nearby Eaton, where soon he became a fixture. Affable and with open eyes and ears, he learned about business strategies while listening to the free-wheeling discussions among local men of affairs. He built a small savings account. Once he tried to supplement his income with seasonal harvest work on a nearby farm. This experience only produced sore muscles and humiliation at being out-worked by the farmer's pre-teen children.[33]

All the while, the young idealist continued to view Black America with a jaundiced eye. Encounters with foibles of urban African Americans added to his disgust with the provincialism of the home folks and increased his disillusionment with his race, his despair that it would ever progress, and his conviction that its misery was mostly its own fault. Micheaux's views found ample support among other African Americans of the period, particularly those who had obtained some education but not enough background or experience with the world to understand that the majority of recently freed slaves did not possess the necessary personal requisites, experience, or wherewithal to make the most of the available opportunies.

Portrayals of his protagonists in *The Conquest* and other novels suggest that Micheaux was well read for the time. Throughout the novels, Micheaux's characters refer knowledgeably to current black literature, although often with disguised titles. In *The Wind from Nowhere*, protagonist Martin Eden sends his young Scottish lady friend, Deborah Stewart, a copy of *The Autobiography of an Ex-Colored Man*, published anonymously in 1912 by James Weldon Johnson. In *The Forged Note*, protagonist Sidney Wyeth refers to *Up from Bondage* by "the greatest Negro the race has ever known", a thinly disguised reference to Booker T. Washington's *Up from Slavery*, which appeared in 1902 and was already a classic. Wyeth also tries, while visiting in "Attalia" [Atlanta] to buy a copy of a magazine called "The Climax", which seems to be a disguised title for the National Association of

Colored People's new house organ, "The Crisis". "The Climax" is "edited by a man who used to be a professor of sociology in one of your colleges" named "Derwin", — obviously a pseudonym for W.E.B. DuBois, who had published several major sociological studies of black culture while at Atlanta University and was then the New York editor of "The Crisis". As well, throughout the early pages of *The Conquest*, Micheaux speaks often about his excursions into mainstream culture as a way of educating himself — a way, he clearly believed, that was open to anyone willing to explore it.[34]

 Up from Slavery and W.E.B. DuBois' brilliant and popular *Souls of Black Folks*, which appeared in 1903, provided considerable food for thought in black communities for many years. Editors and pastors encouraged people to read them, and the books' differing philosophies sparked lively discussions in African American communities. Micheaux read them both and thought about what he had read.

 In a perceptive analysis, scholar Joel Williamson writes that these early years of the 20th century marked a turning point for black people, faced now with the rapidly diminishing white accommodation on which Washington had depended. He pointed out that, as a means of attracting white voters, doors of opportunity were closing to African Americans and suggested that Washington and DuBois agreed on many issues: race pride, racial solidarity, development of black business, the value of manual training, and the need for full political and civil rights. The younger DuBois realized, however, that the inter-racial environment had changed. Radical white racists were gaining political power and their agenda included the reduction of black people to super-subordination. DuBois' *Souls of Black Folks* publicly confronted Washington's unwillingness to change with the times. Williamson suggests that when DuBois convened the first meeting of the so-called Niagara Falls Conference in 1905, he intended to provoke dialogue and bring the debate to the general public. At that meeting, the members vowed that black people "should protest vigorously against political, civil, and economic inequality". These views sparked a lively debate in press and pulpit, emanating as they did from a significant cadre of black leaders. Unfortunately, instead of fostering creative dialogue between Washington and the younger DuBois, it caused Washington to feel so threatened by the new movement as to place spies in DuBois' organization.[35]

Micheaux also would have known about the poisonous racist propaganda that poured from the pens of educated white supremacists. These works, couched in pseudo-scientific language and eagerly embraced by the Radical Right, suggested that Negroes were biologically inferior and would naturally perish without regular infusions of white blood. They also intimated that the plight of the Negro was based on his purported immorality, lasciviousness, laziness, shiftlessness, and lack of gumption to get ahead. At least one scholar has argued that this material provided support for Micheaux's personal views on the foibles of his race.[36] This seems unlikely. White supremacists' vitriol was not new to black people, and they have never lived their lives as if this propaganda were factual. Most considered it an unjust annoyance while recognizing that, like all stereotyping, there were minute grains of fact that appeared to support the premises. Oscar Micheaux' body of work shows little curiosity or interest in white society beyond the cordial relationships and a few enduring friendships with Rosebud neighbors, and his first-hand observations about how white homesteaders had worked together to survive on the Rosebud. He appeared to care little about what white people thought of black people, himself included, beyond learning how one might acquire the better things of life that they enjoyed.

Soon he realized that the white world would tolerate limited penetration by "Negroes of the best character" who were willing to play its game. Working at his suburban shoeshine stand, honing his sales ability and congeniality, he studied their world from the perspective of a small businessman seeking ways to advance himself. It was time to close the shoeshine stand and seek new challenges. With human relations skills that he later would perfect as an entrepreneur, he used his contacts in both worlds to wangle a job in the most prestigious field available to black men outside the confines of the black world: that of a Pullman porter.[37]

Although he worked as a porter only a few years, he returned to it whenever he needed to travel or was short of cash. Throughout his life he continued to profit from the contacts he made, the travel opportunities, and the business and educational experiences associated with the work. Black society valued and respected the Pullman porters during those formative years. These men mastered important skills of personal autonomy, business acumen, human relations, and community leadership. The years of portering provided Micheaux with the equivalent of a college education.

In his definitive book on the profession, Jack Santino describes the black Pullman porters who served a wealthy white clientele as emblematic of the golden age of rail transportation. George Pullman, in creating his luxurious sleeper cars leased to major railroad companies, realized that if the cars were comfortable and offered superlative personalized service, he could control the market of the rich, white, long distance traveler. Pullman's leased cars offered considerable advantage and comfort to the traveler because they provided "through" service from coast to coast. Railroad personnel switched the cars from line to line so that the passengers were not required to change trains. A porter was assigned to a car and its passengers for the length of the run, during which he became well acquainted with their individual needs and peculiarities and could provide them with excellent, personalized service.

By using workers whose sole job was to ensure the comfort of the passengers, Pullman provided a unique, original, and superior travel experience that outstripped the competition and offered high profit. After early and unsuccessful attempts to use white conductors and women for this work, he had turned to an untapped source of labor: black men recently freed from slavery. Not only were these men desperate for work but, given their history, Pullman believed they would perform servile and distasteful chores such as cleaning cuspidors and shining shoes. Over time, the courteous, efficient, unobtrusive porter, maintaining "his proper place," came to symbolize the Pullman Company itself.[38]

For the men, the Pullman Company was a way up and out of poverty — the proverbial "only game in town", a game that was both prestigious and ambivalent. The job of porter was institutionalized, well-paying, and dead end. A young black man had no possibility of advancing from portering even though he might on occasion fill in the duties of a conductor by "running in charge", which meant doing all the conductor's work for no increase in pay.[39]

There were compensations: a chance to see the world, the status of professional costume consisting of a neat uniform versus laborer's denims, urbanity and sophistication, as opposed to rural simplicity, and opportunities to mingle with a variety of sophisticated, wealthy, and influential people — not to mention the opportunity to add to one's income by means of tips. The Pullman porters transmitted culture from the cities of both North and South to the country, bringing black communities the latest trends in music and popular culture, and publicizing opportunities for "the race". They heard the latest in jazz and blues music performed by the growing number of fine African American musicians in urban centers. When they returned home, they brought recordings or sheet music that offered the new sounds; they brought news of new trends and opportunities, along with tales of meeting and talking with admired people, even celebrities, on an equal footing through hours of monotonous train travel. Pullman porters distributed black newspapers and literature to remote rural areas, including fliers touting the "good life" somewhere else. They picked up materials in one city and dropped them off at stations on the route where eager black communities waited to hear the latest news. In other words, the porters served as subtle agents of change.[40]

Although Pullman hired many workers, the job of portering was difficult to get. Often newcomers entered the field with the help of already employed relatives or friends. In some cases, working for the company was a family tradition.[41] In *The Conquest*, Micheaux describes in detail his difficulty first in getting hired and then quickly proving he could master the necessary skills to keep the job.[42] On board a train, the porter was a servant as well as the host on his car. Quickly, Micheaux learned that conditions were unjust and that the company had institutionalized racial subservience by regulation and custom. Still, the porter had the duties of a host to his passengers, while performing and projecting the role of servant. From these conflicting roles, he perfected conventional ways to serve his clients and maximize his tips.

In full charge of the car, the porter developed a variety of subtle and important ways of earning tips by manipulating situations to his financial advantage.[43] Rich people, celebrities, and politicians rode the sleeping cars, and thus porters came into contact with a variety of wealthy white people not accessible to black men outside of domestic service. On the cars, the porter was allowed the intimacy of seeing them as they really were. At the very least, he witnessed their behaviors, sins, indiscretions, and occasional tragedies, and sometimes he served as a temporary friend or confidante to a class of people he otherwise would not have encountered.

Relationships with conductors and railroad employees were often problematic, especially in the pre-union days when Micheaux was portering. The conductor, who made roughly twice the salary of the porter, frequently saw him as a threat to a job which was only secured by the rigid color line. Sometimes when porters were "written up", ostensibly by a spotter, the actual spy was the conductor. The porter's survival depended on developing a working agreement with the conductor on his run.[44]

Micheaux described his unwilling collusion with an alcoholic conductor in a widespread scam that consisted of skimming and splitting money from cash fares. Eventually this resulted in disciplinary action and his temporary release from the company, although by applying for work at St. Louis instead of Chicago he could return to the business whenever he needed to work.[45] His detailed account in *The Conquest* of this experience compares well with Santino's research and oral interviews with other porters.

By all accounts, Oscar greatly enjoyed his years on the railroad once he had mastered the series of skills that the trade required. In four months of work, he had banked his first hundred dollars in savings and had seen the greater portion of the east coast as a result of a series of irregular runs east of the Mississippi. His next assignment was a regular run to Portland,

Oregon, that began his lifelong love affair with the "Great Northwest". "There is something fascinating about railroading", he wrote in *The Conquest*:

> ...few men really tire of it. In fact, most men, like myself, rather enjoy it. I never tired of hearing the t-clack of the tracks and the general roar of the train as it thundered over streams and crossings throughout the days and nights across the continent to the Pacific coast. The scenery never grew old, as it was quite varied between Chicago and North Platte. During the summer it is one large garden farm, dotted with numerous cities, thriving hamlets and towns, fine country homes so characteristic of the great middle west, and is always pleasing to the eye....[46]

His descriptions of the country with its scattered towns as it changed from the verdant middle west of green farms to the harshly beautiful, arid grazing lands and merged with the ragged peaks of the Rockies reflect his growing fascination with the country, which he freely compares with material he was currently reading. He identifies the area of Medicine Bow, Wyoming, with Owen Wister's popular novel, *The Virginian*, and writes knowledgeably about the great federally-financed irrigation and reclamation project then being constructed in the Snake River Valley of Idaho west of American Falls. Idaho greatly appealed to Micheaux as a possible home site, especially that beautiful valley, growing verdant and profitable with the now freely available water supply. He filed that information away for possible future reference.[47]

The few years of work as a porter provided the nest egg that he needed. His savings account now held a few thousand dollars. He had seen the country end to end, and become an accomplished student of human nature. He had learned to mingle easily with white people and to defer to their expectations without a loss of self-confidence. He had made contacts with wealthy white men that would be useful later, and he had viewed them in action as they conducted business. He had used layovers profitably to enhance his education, visiting museums, theaters, libraries, and historical sites along the way; and he had examined the burgeoning West and Middle West with a view to land speculation. He also had ample time to read and think and ponder his next steps. It was time to move on. He would become a homesteader: a pioneer, an example and a role model for his race. He would show them how easily it could be done, and how the "Great Northwest" would provide a haven for African Americans with the will to accomplish great things.

CHAPTER 3
A PRAIRIE VENTURE

During his brief Pullman career, Oscar Micheaux had used every opportunity to observe the American countryside from coast to coast, always with an eye to future speculation. Reluctantly, he had determined that Iowa land was too expensive and Idaho land too arid. Now it was April, 1904, and during a stopover in Council Bluffs, Iowa, he heard a casual conversation in a restaurant between two men, one black, the other white. They were discussing land speculation opportunities in "Oristown", South Dakota [Bonesteel].

> "And where is Oristown?" I inquired, taking a stool and studying the bill of fare.
> "Oristown," the white man spoke up... "is about 250 miles northwest of here in southern South Dakota on the edge of the Little Crow [Rosebud] reservation."[48]

Immediately interested, Micheaux pressed for further information. He learned that the town in question was the terminus of the Chicago and Northwestern Railroad and that it was on the east edge of South Dakota's Rosebud Reservation, which was to be opened by lottery to homestead settlement that fall. Registration for the lottery would begin in July. While his informants allowed that some of the land was arid and unsuitable for farming, other portions were reputed to be of outstanding quality. As soon as he could, he wrote the Department of the Interior in Washington for a prospectus, which he studied carefully.

The land described in the government pamphlets indeed appeared to be what Oscar sought. In many places the soil was a deep black loam with clay subsoil. Rainfall had averaged 28 inches over the past five years, slightly less than the 30 inch average in Iowa. The dryer climate appealed to him because he believed that farm techniques there would be similar to those he had unwillingly learned as a youth in Illinois. There was already some farming experience in the area, largely involving white men who had come to the forts or reservations with the military or as government employees and had stayed to farm. The last killing drought had ended in 1894 and optimists hoped it had been a rare phenomenon. The land in Gregory County was particularly suitable for the type of agriculture Micheaux wished to practice. As he pointed out, all the crops grown in the central west could be produced there while "200 miles north, corn would not mature, 200 miles south, spring wheat is not grown, 200 miles west, the altitude is too high to insure sufficient rainfall to produce a crop, but the reservation lands are in such a position that winter wheat, spring wheat, oats, rye, corn, flax, and barley do well".[49]

"Rosebud country" originally defined the boundaries of a reservation designated for the great Sioux Chief Spotted Tail's Brule band.[50] Located along the Nebraska border, it included the South Dakota counties of Gregory, Tripp, Todd, and Bennett, and portions of Mellette and Washabaugh counties south of the White River. Land in Nebraska north of the Niobrara and KehaPaha rivers also was within its boundaries. Because Spotted Tail (1823-1882) had been determined to protect his young men from the ideas of the accommodationist bands along the Missouri River, not to mention the temptations of gambling, liquor, and loose women readily available at the whiskey stations in the area, he had continually moved his people west. The agency headquarters was relocated to accommodate him, finally coming to rest near Rosebud Creek in Todd County where it remains today. In spring the area around Rosebud Creek boasted an unusual abundance of the pink wild roses common to the Great Plains. Here the Indians would hold their post-hunt feasts, gathering the tender rosebuds and extracting the juice which was seasoned and

thickened with flour, creating a delicate and savory dessert, much prized by the Sioux. Gradually the name Rosebud attached itself to the larger area.[51]
    Either good luck or the intervention of Providence was with Micheaux as he made the choice of location. Within five years numerous places on reservations were opened for settlement by outsiders. The Sioux Agreement of 1889 had defined the boundaries of five reservations for Lakota and Yanktonais people west of the Missouri River.[52] On each of these, federal employees persuaded tribal residents to surrender traditional communalism for landed capitalism in personal allotments to be used for farming or ranching. After the residents began to occupy their allotments, officials encouraged them to sell large unallotted acreages as "surplus" to raise cash to support their new family farming or ranching interests. During the period 1905-1916 opportunities for settlement on surplus acreage opened at remote areas on the Cheyenne River and Standing Rock reservations, at the west end of the Lower Brule Reservation, and on three locations at the east end of the Rosebud Reservation. Any except the Rosebud would have positioned Micheaux on land of little value for agriculture or in a cultural circumstance inhospitable to an immigrant black bachelor. The opening in Gregory County was among the first to be authorized. It was approved by Congress in an act passed on April 23, 1904 (33 *Stat.,* 254).[53]
    Gregory County was located in an area relinquished by a heterogeneous society of tribes more intermarried with outsiders than was any other in all of Lakota Country. For one thing, the county contained the site of the Whetstone Agency where, prior to 1878, accomodationist Indians had gathered near the Missouri River away from Spotted Tail's larger traditionalist following. In the Whetstone group in 1873 lived 65 white men with Native American wives. The whites had come from England, Ireland, Sweden, France, Prussia, Mexico, and Canada. Some had been in residence as long as 26 years. They raised 157 mixed-blood, multi-lingual, multi-cultural children. The Indian mothers mainly were followers of Swift Bear, whose group included some Cheyennes, some Oglalas, and most of all, the "Loafers" — an accommodationist group of mixed tribal extraction. At the urging

of federal officials, they had begun to acculturate to white ways: farming, accepting federal regulations, and accommodating intrusions by a great variety of outside influences.[54]

Even the separatist following of Spotted Tail, which kept its distance at 30 to 70 miles west of the Missouri River, was one of "international" Indian composition. Overall, the most numerous Upper Brules comprised no more than 45 per cent of the population. Others were Miniconjous, Oglalas, Two Kettles, Loafers, and an extraneous group called "Wazhazhes".[55] Gregory County also contained Fort Randall, which through the period 1856-1896 accommodated U.S. Army military and civilian personnel. Some fort personnel always had been African Americans, including the 25th Infantry — the famed African American Buffalo Soldiers who garrisoned the fort from 1880-1884. Micheaux could not have found a group of greater ethnic complexity with more contact with black people anywhere on the Great Plains.

The capacity of long-time residents to accept his arrival was important to his success. Needless to say, his own experience with inter-cultural accommodation was equally significant. Neither the composition of the resident society nor the prior experiences of Micheaux could have tempered the surprise of newcomers after 1904, but his acceptance by "old timers" had the potential to alter the racial attitudes of those who moved in to settle beside him. In any case, Oscar Micheaux could not have discovered a cultural climate in an area opened to settlement better suited to accept the appearance of a lone black man. Surely luck or Providence was on his side.

Although the land where Micheaux would make his home had already begun to acquire the accoutrements of civilization with the arrival of the Chicago and Northwestern Railroad in Bonesteel in 1901, much of the "wild west" remained. Definitely, the Rosebud was Indian country. Just four years prior to its opening to homesteaders, a government report had explained that it was divided into seven districts, each with a non-Indian "boss farmer" whose job was to turn these roaming hunters into agriculturalists. He was assisted by Indian employees. Two mission boarding schools and 21 day schools provided local elementary and trade school education to Indian children and youth. Sioux children who showed outstanding promise were removed from the reservation and schooled elsewhere in the country. Usually the day schools and the issue houses that dispensed supplies and commodities would be in close proximity, becoming the nucleus for small communities that often included a church and a dance hall where pioneers and Indians mingled freely. The few scattered white children were allowed to attend the day schools.[56]

With the Indians confined to reservations and forbidden by the 1862 Treaty of Fort Laramie to hunt for food, a huge opportunity developed to provide meat to the government for issue to the reservation populations. The Bureau of Indian Affairs soon agreed that raising cattle on or near the reservations made more economic sense than driving the animals in from Texas. As a result, large cattle companies leased government land and grazed their cattle on the nutritious grass. Cattle not required on the reservations were driven to market. Before the arrival of the railroad in Bonesteel they were driven to the nearest railroad in Nebraska, but when the Chicago and Northwestern railhead reached Bonesteel in 1901 — and later as it continued westward — small towns along its route became important cattle shipping points. The big cattle drives of 1902, 1906, and 1910 kept the towns booming and kept alive the businesses designed to separate free-spending cowboys from their hard-earned cash.

A scant 50 miles east of the land Micheaux would choose was the Missouri River which, despite the coming of the railroad, remained an important transportation option for travelers of all descriptions. Issue stations where Indians came for rations and steamboat landings all along the river continued to provide for the new homesteaders as well. Closest were landings at Fort Randall and Whetstone, both important refueling stops for steamboats which stopped to take on firewood and to move loads of cattle, grain and other products to markets up and down the river.

Although many Sioux were modestly successful at cattle ranching, they regarded farming with a jaundiced eye, remarking that "God made the earth right side up." Farmers who arrived with Micheaux during the wet cycle might have done better to listen to the Indians and local white farmers who had grown virtually nothing during the last dry cycle. Nevertheless, during the early years of the twentieth century, emphasis was on farming, and both Indians and white homesteaders would participate.[57]

As in earlier days, the now limited remaining opportunities for homesteading in Micheaux's "Great Northwest" provided the best hope for people of modest means to acquire property. The fundamental principle of homestead law was to provide acreage to any person of legal age who would comply with the basic requirements. Many potential homesteaders were not farmers and were more interested in speculation than in creating permanent homes. These people believed that six months of "constructive residence" involving breaking a few acres and building a shelter plus payment of a few dollars was small price to pay for a stairstep to riches.

To provide fair and widespread access to coveted and diminishing homestead lands, the government resorted to a lottery system that sparked intense interest. Oscar Micheaux learned that this was the manner in which the Gregory County lands would be dispensed. Registering for the drawing was simple. A person desiring to register for 160 acres went before a notary public at one of the registration points and completed the government forms that were collected in a huge canvas bag. On drawing day, a blindfolded child drew out the numbers one at a time. The person drawing #1 had first choice of all the land. Usually holders of the numbers secured the services of a locator, one of hundreds who professed to know the country thoroughly and for a nominal fee would take the applicant out to look at land. Once the selection was made, the homesteader went to the land office and filed an entry on the desired piece of land. Those who filed the first three months would pay $4 per acre; the second, $3, and after that the price was $2.50 per acre.[58] There would be 2,400 parcels of land available in Gregory County and the drawing was scheduled to occur in Chamberlain in late summer 1904. To be eligible, Micheaux must appear at one of the three registration sites in July and complete the necessary papers. The sites included Yankton in the southeastern corner of the state and Chamberlain in central South Dakota, both on the Missouri River. Bonesteel, the third site, was in Gregory County but was one of the most notorious wide open towns in the west, equal in reputation to Dodge City or Deadwood. As a cattle shipping point, it had long attracted the free-spending cowboys drawn to the gambling parlors, saloons, and ladies of the night. Controlled by a gang of gamblers and thugs, the town provided little protection for law abiding citizens. It was axiomatic that when Pinkerton Detectives were looking for a shady character they started at Bonesteel, where they usually found him.[59]

As a lone black man in unfamiliar territory, not looking for trouble, Micheaux decided to bypass Bonesteel. Instead, he chose to register at Chamberlain ["Johnstown" in *The Conquest*], conveniently served by three railroads.[60] There, accommodations were supposedly more adequate and protection from the criminal element more efficient.

When he arrived on July 5, 1904, he found the town severely overcrowded with registrants, mostly from other states in the Midwest. Making his way through the throng, he selected one of the numerous notary booths and completed his registration papers. Later he described his astonishment at the crowds of people with identical goals. Within hours of his arrival his certainty that he would emerge from the drawing with a chance for a prime location was badly shaken. Obviously competition would be fierce. Throngs of people were pouring into Chamberlain, and by the end of the week he believed that at least 75,000 people had registered. Later he learned from a Kansas City paper that the final registration totaled 107,000. He figured now that his odds were 1 in 44. When he received his notification from the Superintendent that he had drawn #6504, he knew he had lost. He learned this depressing news on "the same day that I had lost $54 out of my pocket...[which combination of news] gave me the grouch and I lit out for the Louisiana Purchase Exposition at St. Louis with the intention of returning to Pullman service...".[61]

This time he obtained a prestigious run between New York and the fair, and the tips were excellent. He managed to save over three hundred dollars running from September 1 to October 4. Remembering what he had learned in Dakota about the possibility for purchase of a relinquishment, Oscar returned to his dream of securing a Dakota homestead.[62]

Relinquishments were lands returned to the market for sale by claim holders for a variety of reasons including death or abandonment. Prices varied with the quality and location and the eagerness of the buyer or seller. Traffic in relinquishments became the largest stock-in-trade of the real estate dealers and speculators.

A trip to Bonesteel was now a necessity, but it had become a somewhat safer venture. On August 18, 1904, about six weeks before his arrival, the law abiding citizens reached the breaking point. Accompanied by the sheriff, they advised the gamblers to close their illegal operations or leave town. The result was the "Battle of Bonesteel" during which the gamblers were forced at gunpoint to take the next train out of town. One gambler was killed in the fracas and people on both sides were injured. Now it appeared that law and order might have a chance, and although drinking and gambling remained, the lawless elements had lost control of the government.[63]

Feeling somewhat better about his personal safety, Micheaux traveled from Omaha on the Chicago and Northwestern Railroad's single daily train crowded with other potential purchasers, arriving on October 4, 1904. As the only African American on the train, he was the object of much curiosity and regarded as something of a joke. Indeed, on arrival in the town still bursting with transients eager to buy relinquishments and with confidence men waiting to exploit them, he had difficulty finding a land agent to take him seriously.

Finally he found a livery stable owner and part-time agent who agreed to take him to visit prospective sites. En route, the man confided that he had been called a fool for "wasting his time hauling a damn nigger around because he obviously had no money and was just stalling". Angrily Micheaux replied,

> "Show me what I want and I will produce the money. What I want is something near the west end of the county. You say the relinquishments are cheaper there and the soil is richer. I don't want big hills or rocks or anything I can't farm, but I want a nice level or gently rolling quarter section of prairie,

near some town to be, that has the prospects of getting the railroad when it is extended west from
Oristown." [64]

As they entered the reservation boundary three miles west of
"Oristown", Micheaux, ever the visionary, noted

...the long grass, now dead, which was of a
brownish hue and as I gazed over the miles of it
lying like a mighty carpet I could seem to feel the
magnitude of the development and industry that
would someday replace this state of wildness.[65]

It was wild and beautiful country, this Missouri River valley,
very different from the land of his youth, and it created a hyp-
notic attraction which would remain with Oscar Micheaux for the
rest of his life. His timeless description of the land he saw during
the long buggy ride to his new home still sparks a nostalgic
yearning in the hearts of prairie dwellers.

To the Northeast the Missouri River wound its
way, into which empties the Whetstone Creek, the
breaks of which resembled miniature mountains,
falling abruptly, then rising to a point where the
dark shale sides glistened in the sunlight...We could
go perhaps three or four miles on a table-like
plateau then drop suddenly into small canyon-like
ditches and rise abruptly to the other side....Nine
miles northwest [of the new town of Hedrick
(Herrick)] where the land was sandy and full of pits,
into which the buggy wheels dropped with a grind-
ing sound, and where magnesia rock cropped out of
the soil, was another budding town by the name of
Kirk [Burke]. ...This sandy land continued some
three miles west and we often found springs along
the streams.[66]

The sandy, rocky land around Burke was not at all what Micheaux was seeking, and for a few depressing moments he wondered if he had made a mistake. Then he found it—the land he had dreamed about.

> After ascending an unusually steep hill, we came upon a plateau where the grass, the soil, and the lay of the land were entirely different from any we had as yet seen. I was struck by the beauty of the scenery and it seemed to charm and bring me out of the spirit of depression the sandy stretch brought upon me. Stretching for miles to the northwest and to the south the land would rise in a gentle slope to a hog back, and as gently slope away to a draw, which drained to the south. Here the small streams emptied into a larger one, winding along like a snake's track, and thickly wooded with a growth of small hardwood timber. It was beautiful. From each side the land rose gently like huge wings, and spread away as far as the eye could reach. The driver pointed to the north and announced, "There lays [sic] one of the claims." 67

On the highest point of the claim they located the small square white stone that provided its legal description: "SWC, SWQ, Sec. 29-97-72, W. 5th P.M."

The driver translated this to mean the "southwest corner of the southwest quarter of section 29, township 97, and range 72, west of the 5th principal meridian". The owner was a girl who lived with her parents across the Missouri River. Micheaux and the land man visited her and after some dickering with the claimant and the agent, he concluded his purchase and found himself the proud owner of a Rosebud claim.68

At the time Oscar again was half-heartedly courting Jessie, the young lady from his Chicago days, now a high school senior back home in Illinois. He wrote ecstatically to her about his new purchase and she responded in kind. Secure in the dream that he would soon be a successful farmer and land speculator in the

"Great Northwest" with a beautiful wife to share his good fortune, and with winter approaching, he left the Rosebud to replenish his savings on the railroad, with time out at Christmas to visit his lady-love.[69]

It was Oscar's first semi-serious attempt at courtship, and he was pleased to see that Jessie had grown into an attractive, if inexperienced, young lady. He told her all about his plans in the "Great Northwest" but stopped just short of asking her to marry him, remembering that the wild, lonely plains filled with rough white homesteaders and "wild Indians" was no place for a gently brought up young colored lady. They agreed to continue their correspondence.

Portering was remunerative that season. In addition to a private fall trip to South America serving a group of New York capitalists and millionaires that enriched his education as well as his pocketbook, the winter run from St. Louis to Florida brought excellent tips. Early that spring there was an opening on a regular run to Boston that allowed Micheaux to enjoy a city that had always fascinated him. Knowing that this would be his last trip as a railroad employee for the foreseeable future and realizing that life on the Rosebud would be lonely and isolated, he used this run to soak up as much urban "culture" as he could hold.

The mornings I spent wandering around the city, visiting Faneuil Hall, the Old State House, Boston [C]ommons, Bunker Hill, and a thousand other reminders of the early heroism, rugged courage, and far seeing greatness of Boston's early citizens. Afternoons generally found me on Tremont or Washington Street attending a matinee or hearing music. There once I heard Caruso, Melba, and two or three other grand opera stars in the popular Rigoletto Quartette and another time I witnessed reproduction of the Kishniff Massacre with 200 people on the stage. On my last trip I saw Chauncey Olcott in "Terrence the Coach Boy", a romance of old Ireland with the scene laid in Valley Bay which seemed to correspond to the Back Bay a few blocks away.... Dear old Boston, when will I see you again was my thought as the train pulled out through the most fashionable part of America, so stately and so grand.[70]

It was time to close the door on the wandering life and open the door to a new and challenging world — one where he could match and measure his skills against white homesteaders and prove to himself and to others of his race that indeed, "a colored man could be anything".

CHAPTER 4

THE HOMESTEADER

Most of what we know about Oscar Micheaux's experiences in the "Great Northwest" comes from his own accounts in *The Conquest* and the later novels. By comparing *The Homesteader* and *The Wind from Nowhere* with his original, fresh-told autobiography in *The Conquest*, and with local accounts of Rosebud settlement, it is possible to draw reasonable conclusions about his experiences and his acceptance in the community as well as something about the type of life this solitary black man created for himself in the new land.

In *The Conquest* he continues his story by revealing that in early April, 1905, he boarded the train at St. Louis for his new home on the Rosebud. Although he had just left Jessie and was feeling a little lonely, he was full of optimism, bolstered by the $3,000 nest egg that would start him on his farming venture. His agent met him at Bonesteel with the welcome news that a town called "Calais" [Dallas] was being built just south of his homestead. Already word had spread that the "colored man" who had taken up land the previous year and had not yet returned surely would reconsider and be willing to sell. Within minutes of their meeting, the agent offered him a profitable sale which he declined. Instead, he departed Bonesteel the next morning on Brown Dad Burpee's stage line, noticing en route that new wooden buildings had appeared in the towns of Herrick and Burke.

The new town of Dallas, perched atop a hill, soon appeared on the horizon and was the scene of bustling activity. Micheaux's arrival occasioned considerable comment, for the appearance of the "colored" homesteader aroused much curiosity. A Bonesteel acquaintance immediately took him to meet the town leaders: the postmaster and the president of the Western Townsite Company whose firm was the primary developer of the site. "Ernest Nicholson" [Ernest Jackson] was one of the most powerful men on the Rosebud. Oscar Micheaux was a sufficient judge of human relations to grasp the importance of this meeting.

> I could see at a glance that here was a person of unusual aggressiveness and great capacity for doing things. As he looked at me his eyes seemed to bore clear through, and as he asked a few questions his searching look would make a person tell the truth whether he would or no...That evening at the hotel he asked me whether I wished to double my money by selling my relinquishment. "No," I answered, "but I tell you what I do want to do... I am not here to sell; I am here to make good or die trying; I am here to grow up with this country and prosper with the growth if possible. I have a little coin back in old 'Chi'... and when these people begin to commute and want to sell I am ready to buy another place." ...I admired the fellow. He reminded me of "the richest man in the world" in "The Lion and The Mouse", Otis Skinner as Colonel Phillippi Brideau, an officer on the staff in Napoleon's Army in "The Honor of the Family" and other characters in plays that I greatly admired where courage, strength of character and firm decision were displayed....[71]

Ernest Jackson and his brothers, Frank and Graydon, were sons of Frank D. Jackson, who had been governor of Iowa from 1894-1896. They had family ties to Chicago and Northwestern Railroad magnate Marvin Hughett, a man whose decisions about the location of railroad lines in South Dakota were critical. The senior Jackson owned the Royal Union Insurance Company and was sufficiently wealthy to provide financial backing to his sons in their real estate development and other business ventures. Over the next twenty years the sons would establish a number of towns on the Rosebud, including Lamoreaux, Dallas, Winner, Carter, and Colome. In addition to the townsite development ventures, the

Jackson brothers owned banks and later developed two of the largest cattle ranches on the Rosebud. One of these, the Mulehead, established in 1912 at a location thirteen miles northeast of Bonesteel, eventually comprised 169,000 acres and used 60 men to manage over 11,000 Hereford cattle, some of which were driven to Bonesteel and shipped to Sioux City or Omaha on the railroad. The Mulehead was destined to become a showplace with a reputed investment by the Jackson brothers of over $3,000,000. It included modern housing for the ranch manager and the workers as well as its own electric generating plant. A second large Jackson-owned ranch appeared near Winner at about the same time.[72]

Micheaux's experience serving men like the Jacksons on the railroad and as a private porter helped him during this initial meeting. Evidently he passed muster, for throughout the homesteading accounts — and later in the memories of locals — there is evidence that one or another of the Jacksons stood by him, apparently in friendship, with financial advice and assistance. Surely, acceptance by these influential men hastened his acceptance by other white settlers in new country during a time when widespread belief in black inferiority was virtually a given. Oscar Micheaux was off to a good start with that aspect of his adventure. Other aspects would prove to be more problematic.

In *The Conquest* Oscar recounted his perils with humor, but at the time they must have been more painful than funny. Some of these mistakes survive in well-embroidered family stories passed down by early residents and told today with a great deal of earnestness by their descendants.[73]

Listening to these tales couched in the careful, politically correct language of the late nineteen nineties and recounted at Micheaux festivals in the sometimes daunting presence of black scholars from east and west coasts, one is struck by their unwitting reflection of racial myths common to the period. Micheaux and his white neighbors, acutely aware of prevailing social prejudices associated with racial differences, were playing the "race game". Local memories appear to agree with Micheaux's comments that, no matter how comfortable he became with his neighbors, he remained conscious of his race and understood always that white acceptance was capricious. For example, some recall that he rarely sat at table with his white neighbors although he loved the fresh-baked goods pressed on him by the farm wives who worried about the lonely bachelor.[74] One might speculate that he applied this convention selectively, depending on his perception of his white companions' egalitarianism, since he spoke of "boarding" with the family of "the Scottish girl".

Sometimes the deceptively subtle humor of a race accustomed to "having white folks on", delivered by Micheaux with the appearance of great seriousness, seemed to escape the white settlers, especially the children — who really believed that a recalcitrant cow was going to be "beaten half to death" if it didn't change its ways.[75] On the other hand, "nigger" and other racial or ethnic epithets were "household words", carelessly used throughout the Midwest by Indians, native-born white Americans, and immigrants, and not necessarily connoting insult. And, in this melting pot of people from many American and European backgrounds, settlers who observed ethnic customs or habits different from their own might make caustic comments that, while hurtful, were often more thoughtless than accurate or dangerous.

Micheaux, however, was born and raised in the ambiguous social climate of southern Illinois. For all of his young life he had walked the delicate balance between black and white worlds, always slightly uncomfortable in both. He had learned that a misstep could spell disaster or even death. Although he might have been comfortable enough with the Jacksons and their ilk, for "place" with dignity was a skill he had mastered, the European immigrants and their white counterparts from the American Midwest represented a treacherous unknown. Thus, in Micheaux's writings, as well as the neighbors' stories, one finds reflections of the lingering cultural misunderstanding common to people who were struggling to make sense of each other.

For the youthful Micheaux, the years on the Rosebud were a time of learning new human relations skills as well as new farming skills, a tenuous time of testing and experimentation that would eventually build a few quiet, lasting friendships not always acknowledged in the separatist years before the civil rights movement. Perhaps this is one reason why the mature Micheaux returned repeatedly to the Rosebud and his homesteading experiences in his films and writings throughout his life.

Some interesting critical impressions of Oscar Micheaux have
lingered among South Dakotans, exacerbated after his departure
and later success in the film industry during a time when his former neighbors suffered in depression and drought. For example,
some, unaware of the carefully masked but constant financial
struggles dogging his success, remained convinced that he was
the consummate opportunist. His early choice of land so close to
the town of Dallas, as well as his later land purchases were, they
believed, blatantly speculative and based on his probable inside
information about the workings of the railroad industry.[76] This
theory ignored the fact that a railroad porter was probably not in
possession of much inside management information and blithely
disregarded the truth that many, if not most, of the homesteaders
were engaged in similar speculation. Indeed, the evidence,
including his insistence on purchasing high quality farm land, suggests that land speculation was a very important part of
Micheaux's carefully planned future. First, however, it would be
necessary to succeed on the original homestead.

Settling into his new life, he hired a sod mason with carpen-
ter skills from Herrick who, for three dollars a day, helped him
build

> a frame barn large enough for three horses; a sod
> house sixteen by fourteen with a hip roof made of
> two by fours for rafters, and plain boards with tar
> paper and sod with the grass turned downward and
> laid side by side, the cracks being filled with sand.
> The house had two small windows and one door
> that was a little short on account of my getting tired
> of carrying sod. I ordered the "contractor" to put the
> roof on as soon as I felt it was high enough to be
> comfortable inside. The fifth day I moved in. There
> was no floor but the thick, short buffalo grass made
> a neat carpet. In one corner I put the bed, while in
> another I set the table, [in] the one next the door I
> placed the stove, a little two-hole burner gasoline
> [stove], and in the other corner I made a bin for the
> horses' grain.[77]

Reluctantly, Oscar had learned to farm in Illinois but now the prospect did not seem unpleasant. He was, after all, doing it his own way for himself. Like most Dakota greenhorns, he made his share of mistakes, in full view of his neighbors who had no idea what to make of him. He soon learned that breaking new land required enormous physical strength and that the "gummy" West River soils were quite different from the easily worked soil of his father's farm. The first task was to plot the new fields carefully, setting the first furrow straight and true. It was important to use the correct kind of plow: a special "breaking plow" with a shaft tough enough to cut through thick masses of deeply rooted grass. His first plow was not adequate. It made a square cut, which caused the roots and grasses to collect on the plow which would not stay in the ground.

> "I hopped, skipped, and jumped across the prairie," he would later recall, "and that plow began hitting and missing, mostly missing. ...Well, I sat down and gave up to a fit of the blues; for it looked bad, mighty bad to me." [78]

Eventually he found the correct plow blade, one which would make a long, slanting cut, cleanly severing the deep grass roots. Progress was then more rapid. Soon he developed a routine in which he would plow two or three rods without stopping to clear the blade, and as he gained skill, he eventually could travel forty rods without mishap. By the end of the summer, he had broken 120 acres, more land than most of his neighbors who were having similar difficulties but were less ambitious or more experienced. Unlike Micheaux, who was desperate to prove himself, they broke sod in smaller areas and got them planted, breaking new land only when time and weather permitted. They understood that the only limits to sod breaking were frozen ground and snow cover. After all, successful crop production was the long-term goal and the annual cycle of farm labor — plowing, planting, cultivating, and harvesting — shaped the daily routine.[79]

One of his most publicly painful learning experiences, recounted in considerable detail in *The Conquest*, dealt with his difficulty in obtaining good work horses. Before he finally found a satisfactory team, every crooked horse trader or horse thief in the area had tried to cheat him (and there were many such unscrupulous dealers in the vicinity of Burke). He tried out a considerable number of horses before he found animals that would suit him, and eventually ended up with a mismatched team of horse and mule. The most interesting aspect of the tale lies in his reaction, for throughout his ordeal he was able to see the humor in the situation. Each day, rain or shine, he went out with his mismatched team and his breaking plow. People stopped to laugh at "the nigger" while they watched his struggle. Their laughter turned eventually to a grudging respect, then to acceptance, and finally to admiration, when they realized that he had broken many more acres of prairie than most of them.[80]

Some of his neighbors' recollections found his unorthodox farming methods highly amusing. For example, they shook their heads at the sight of him "using eight horses pulling a binder with a seeder on behind. Harvesting and seeding at the same time was an innovation all his own".[81]

Oscar watched his neighbors, too, and was struck by their diversity. They ranged from the Missouri spinster on the west to a "loud talking German" further north, and an English preacher near the German. A "big fat lazy barber who seemed to be taking the rest cure joined me on the east...the most uncompromisingly lazy man on the Little Crow". Also in the neighborhood were a merchant and a banker, and others "of all vocations in life, of all nationalities except negroes, and I controlled the colored vote".[82]

As he gained his neighbors' trust, he was eventually able to remark that he never spent a lonely evening. He helped the Missouri spinster provide direction to her plowman that saved her crop. During the winter he used his spare time to haul coal and other supplies from the railhead at Bonesteel to Dallas for his neighbors and Dallas businessmen.[83] In *The Conquest* he described returning from such a trip in the middle of a "genuine South Dakota blizzard", material he later used in the opening scenes of the semi-fictional *Homesteader*. By the middle of the first winter he was ready for a change and, leaving his livestock in good hands, he went back to the railroad for several months, with time out to pursue his courtship of Jessie who had been ill. Apparently the romance was proceeding apace until he returned to the Rosebud and the strain of separation caused jealousy to get the better of him. Instead of facing the issue squarely, he gave it up, ceased their correspondence, and returned to tending his crops.[84] Like other young men's, Oscar's interest in girls tended to be sporadic and half-hearted until finally he fell in love.

Crops were good those early years. Mostly unaware of the treacherous and deceptive weather cycles common to the Great Plains, farmers had hurried to capitalize on their early success by purchasing additional land and indulging in widespread booster-ism. There was no more enthusiastic booster than Oscar Micheaux. On his annual trips to Chicago, Kansas, and southern Illinois he never missed a chance to encourage other African Americans to try the "Great Northwest". Frequently he was disappointed by their lack of enthusiasm.

By 1910, Oscar was honing his writing skills in articles describing opportunities in South Dakota and submitting them to the eastern press. On March 19, 1910, the five year old *Chicago Defender*, destined to become the premier midwestern voice for Black America, published "Where the Negro Fails". In this lengthy article, Oscar Micheaux reminded young black readers of Horace Greeley's admonition to "go west, young man, and grow up with the country." He chastised them for their lack of foresight in recognizing opportunity and their "inability to see common sense in looking to the future".[85]

Castigating the race for these faults was a common theme during the early 20th century, echoed by editors and race leaders alike, including the outspoken W.E.B. DuBois who, while recognizing his people's lethargy, tempered his criticism by asserting that blaming the victim was an over-simplification. Unlike other critics, DuBois argued that it would take more than "gumption" to extricate a mostly willing but ill-prepared black peasantry from their depths of poverty and despair.[86]

Despite African Americans' lack of interest in the Rosebud, the country continued to grow. Enthusiastic farmers pressured town leaders and state politicians to get the railroad extended quickly. Railroad competition was hindered by the difficulty of bridging the Missouri River, whose soft bottom and ever-changing channels did not bode well for successful bridging. Very likely the Chicago and Northwestern Railroad, which bypassed the river by entering the state from Nebraska, would remain the "only game in town" and everyone hoped it would be extended soon. The only matters for speculation were the time frame and the route. For the many small towns, the route was literally a question of life or death. A town bypassed soon became a town dead. Well-heeled townsite developers, competing among themselves, and aware that the steam engines needed stops to replenish fuel and water approximately every ten miles, ensured that villages were created to cover every possible route. These savvy and close-mouthed developers also knew that Tripp County, immediately to the west, soon would open to settlement. All of these facts, as well as competition among the towns for the permanent county seat, created a heady mixture of local politics on which individual fortunes would rise or fall. Each settler prayed he or she had guessed right and chosen a homestead with easy access to the railhead town or the seat of local government.

Oscar Micheaux followed these developments with great interest, expecting, of course, that Dallas would come out a winner despite the fact that the most touted route followed the government-platted towns of Herrick, Burke, and Gregory well to the north. That scenario meant Gregory would become the new railhead in time to take full advantage of the impending Tripp County opening. Naturally the merchants and boosters in the three towns promoted this to their advantage. On the other hand, it was in Bonesteel's best interest to delay the extension of the railhead as long as possible.

Meantime, the Jackson brothers who had developed Dallas quietly circulated the "sure fire intelligence" that the railroad would proceed directly from Bonesteel to Dallas before reaching a terminus at Gregory. Micheaux's property was located immediately north of Dallas. Such a development could mean his land might eventually become city lots. Others in town who knew that his calamitous horse dealings had been expensive were sure that the "lone negro" would sell out cheap and leave the country well before a boom. It was the kind of implied dare Micheaux could not resist. Instead of selling out, he used the remainder of his savings to buy another parcel of land, bringing his total holdings to 320 acres. In April 1907, just when he was beginning to wonder how he would manage the payments, word came that the railroad surveyors had arrived in Bonesteel.

In the next weeks, as it became increasingly certain that the route would follow the government towns and miss Dallas, panicked townspeople looked around for their leader, Ernest Jackson, the loudest booster of Dallas, who was nowhere to be found. In his absence, enterprising boosters from Gregory enticed a few Dallas businessmen away — together with their easily moved wooden buildings — and prepared to capitalize on their victory. Meantime, the Jacksons had established an office in Gregory and when Ernest quietly returned to town after his unsuccessful lobbying trip to the Chicago railroad magnates, the brothers offered to move their entire business holdings to a new Gregory headquarters.

Then, Micheaux recounted, Gregory "made the most stupid mistake of her life". In the flush of victory, the town fathers insulted the Jacksons by strongly suggesting that their business headquarters was not needed assure the town's success. Quietly, Ernest went away on another trip. It would be winter before he returned.

In his absence, Dallas commercial buildings, including the town's best hotel, continued to be carted off to Gregory. To the dismay of Dallas residents, all that remained of the business district were the buildings owned by the Jacksons: "the old two-story frame hotel, a two-story bank, the saloon, drug store, their own office, and a few smaller ones". Not only were the townspeople inconvenienced, they were forced to endure the gloating of Gregory citizens while viewing with dismay the booming land development in Gregory just five miles away.

Gregory, however, had reckoned without Ernest Jackson. Micheaux continues the story:

> I was at the depot in Oristown the day he arrived. There he boarded an auto and went west to Megory. On his arrival there, he ordered John Nogden to proceed to Calais, load the bank building, get all the horses obtainable, and proceed at once to haul the bank to—no, not to Megory—this is what the Megoryites thought when, with seventy-six hors-

es hitched to it, they saw the bank of Calais coming toward Megory. But when it got to within a half a mile of the south side, swerved off to the west. About six that evening, when the sun went down, the Bank of Calais was sitting on the side of a hill that sloped to the north, near the end of the survey.[87]

The Jacksons' bank was open for business the next day. Reactions ranged from hilarity to mystification to panic. Over the next 60 days, a genial Ernest Jackson kept his own counsel and continued to move his buildings. Court records showed that someone was quietly buying up property west of Gregory and paying top prices for it, too. Before long it was obvious that Jackson know-how had triumphed. The new town would become New Calais (New Dallas). County historians reported in 1913 that officially it came into being on April 20, 1907.[88] Now the reincarnated Dallas had become the gateway to Tripp County and on August 18, 1907, the Chicago and Northwestern Railroad arrived.

When the dust settled, Ernest regaled his friend, Oscar, with the story. Incensed that the town fathers of Gregory had spurned their offer of cooperation, Jackson had marshalled his business and family connections in Omaha and Des Moines, and then traveled to Chicago where they made the case that western cattle ranchers would prefer railroad access through a less settled area than that around Gregory. The result was a private deal with Marvin Hughett of the Chicago and Northwestern Railroad, and the deed was done.[89]

With Dallas and Gregory now in cut-throat competition for control of both commerce and land development, a wild boom began. Years of bumper crops in the central Midwest had left farmers with money to invest and a crop of youthful native and immigrant farmers looking to buy. Bumptious Dakota boosters spread the word of land bargains far and wide. The Jackson brothers were riding high, flushed with the victory over Gregory and still backed by their father's money. Competing towns initiated price wars over milling and elevator fees as well as prices on goods sold by local merchants. The two-cylinder automobile had reached the Rosebud. Now potential buyers could be driven across bumpy terrain to view the land before being taken back to one of the competing towns for free dinner and lodgings in a "luxury" hotel. Because Tripp County remained closed, the newest expansion was occurring immediately north of Gregory and Dallas. Crops were lush and profitable, silent tribute to the wet cycle that remained in full sway. The land had never looked more inviting.

Oscar Micheaux had moved his post office box to Gregory and remained interested and involved in the bustle and excitement. Land agents handled their potential buyers with great care, ensuring that they saw only the best portions of the tracts and steering them clear of disgruntled and frustrated settlers. Micheaux was known as a successful homesteader and an eloquent booster. He loved to visit with the outsiders, and his travel on the railroads as well as his homesteading experience gave him plenty to talk about. Moreover, as a successful "colored farmer", he appeared as a unique example of success for white prospects who reasoned, "if he can do it - of COURSE I can...".

The railroad had brought African American dining car waiters and Pullman porters into the country along with transient black hotel porters, cooks, and waiters. Ever hopeful that his race would see in the "Great Northwest" what he had seen, Micheaux tried without success to convince them to purchase land and cast their lot with him. He knew from visits to his family in rural Kansas that black homesteaders were succeeding well as serious agriculturalists, but he was never able to sell this success story to the transient members of his race; and he never could understand why. Sadly, he reported in *The Conquest*, during this whole period he was able to secure the registration of only one "colored man" — his oldest brother.[90]

Congress passed the Tripp County Homestead Act on March 2, 1907 (24 *Stat.* 1230). Part of a national program, it gave persons throughout the United States the opportunity to select homesteads within the county after tribal members and their families had chosen their allotments or homesites. The county's formal recognition by President Theodore Roosevelt followed on August 26, 1908, and set forth the terms, conditions, and procedures that would be used to open the settlement process.[91] The land would be expensive — $6 an acre — but that did not deter potential buyers, nor the grafters, con men, gamblers, and opportunists eager to exploit them. It would be Bonesteel all over again, this time split between Dallas and Gregory. More than 115,000 people would register for Tripp County lands. With 320 acres, Micheaux was well on the way to his goal of owning 1000. He had every intention of investing, but he knew prices and choice would be better when relinquishments became available.

The account in *The Conquest* of the Jacksons' triumph over Gregory and the subsequent events of settlement is very detailed and accurate. Scholars Pearl Bowser and Louise Spence theorize that "although his 'objective reporting' of the details and key players obviously attempts to distance Micheaux from these speculators, it is given such prominence in an otherwise personal story that one cannot help but wonder what role he had in the scheme. Indeed, the image of Micheaux as land speculator seems more in tune with Micheaux-the-entrepreneur than with Micheaux-the-homesteader".[92]

The settlement of Tripp County proved as dramatic as events in Gregory. The first town in the county was Lamoreaux, named after a mixed-blood [Indian-white] family and shortened by the Post Office to Lamro. Because it was first, its citizens were positive that it would be the next stop for the Chicago and Northwestern Railroad. They had reckoned without the intrepid Jacksons, whose Western Townsite Company had an arrangement with the Chicago and Northwestern Railroad to plat towns all along a potential railroad right of way. Western had subcontracted much of the work to the Pioneer Townsite Company, a subsidiary of the railroad, and tasked to do the railroad's bidding. Thus, when Pioneer developed the town of Winner, Lamro lost the railroad but hoped to capture the county seat. Other towns sprang up across the prairie: Jordan, McNeeley, Carter, Clearfield, Ideal, Hammil, Witten, Colome.... Four of them (Lamro, Winner, Colome, and Witten) were involved in the bloody battle for the permanent county seat. Much was at stake. The county seat, home of county government including tax collection, guaranteed that virtually every county citizen would be required to visit the town at least once a year. County seats inevitably prospered.

Again Winner emerged victorious, and the results sparked another stealthy move of buildings and county records from Lamro to Winner.[93] Soon Lamro became a ghost town.

It was no accident that Micheaux's fictitious designation for Winner was "Victor". His enthusiastic and detailed reporting of these events indicates a lively interest, personal commitment to the Rosebud, and his widespread acceptance as a respected member of the community. Oscar apparently enjoyed the Winner area. Over time, he would acquire three Tripp County homesteads and use Winner as his primary trading center, patronizing the town's businesses. Local historian Lee Arlie Barry recorded that he sometimes earned extra cash by working as an occasional janitor in the Molosh Saloon in downtown Winner.[94] Perhaps he drew on those experiences when writing about his male protagonists who frequently enjoyed "answering the call of the wild" by spending evenings in the local frontier saloons.

An essentially private man, Oscar Micheaux knew many different people and much more about life on the Rosebud than he might have cared to share in his books. As he gradually acquired and farmed more land in widely scattered locations, locals noted and remembered the tall, long-legged, athletic black man striding across the prairie en route to town or to one of his farmsteads. These frequent treks in all weather necessarily led to unusual encounters and odd friendships that might not have been publicly discussed. As a "marginal" individual, outnumbered by white settlers, he was aware of and interested in other "marginal" people, including other blacks and those whites who were rumored to have Indian or "colored" blood but who disavowed it.

For example, he could hardly have resided in South Dakota during the homestead period without being aware of the large Sully County Colored Colony thriving not far to the northeast. Begun in Fairbanks Township on the banks of the Missouri River northeast of Pierre in 1884 by Norval Blair, an ex-slave from northern Illinois, and his adult children, it had prospered. During the homestead boom of 1905-1910, a number of African American families tried their luck in western Sully County, and by the 1910 census, the immediate area was home to at least 13 black homesteading families. Norval's son, Ben, and daughter, Betty, were well known throughout the state as African American leaders who had joined with the black citizens of Yankton in 1906 to explore ways to attract black settlers "of the best class" to choose homes in South Dakota.

In the far southeast corner of the state, the sizeable African American Yankton colony, begun in the 1880s by steamboat workers, consisted mainly of artisans, laborers, and small farmers. It was large enough during Micheaux's early years on the Rosebud to support both a Baptist and a Methodist church.

Closer to home, Jim and Mary Stark were siblings who homesteaded together a few miles south of Burke on the Nebraska border at Jamison, where Mary was active in the local Methodist Church and both were well regarded in the community.

In nearby northwestern Nebraska, a small homesteading community of African Americans took up farms in the marginally productive sand hills near Brownlee under provisions of the Kincaid Act. That colony, some of whose members prospered, might have included light complexioned families that Micheaux would later describe as "passing" for white.

When Tripp County opened for settlement, black residents included the Gary brothers, Bruce and Solomon. Bruce was a mail carrier. Solomon and his wife taught in the Little Crow School at Mosher, one of the many settlements in the area. Another African American was a former Civil War nurse, Susie Bird. She is described in the Tripp County histories as a pleasant, competent, and elegant black woman who delivered babies for homesteaders and Indians alike.[95]

Mainly, Micheaux's writings are silent about the presence of these people except in the context of individuals who appeared to have deserted their heritage and were passing for white. The fact, however, that he returned frequently to the Rosebud experience for film plots that included black people, coupled with his obvious lively interest in all aspects of his surroundings, argues strongly for his awareness of at least some of these people who might well have been prospects for the sale of his books.

Likewise, he necessarily would have known more about Rosebud Indian people than he shared in his writings. Stories from white Rosebud families, collected and published in the plethora of county histories that emerged in honor of the 1976 bicentennial, are replete with tales about interactions between the settlers and their Indian neighbors, many suggesting regular cordial contact. Yet, in his writings, Micheaux referred to the numerous Sioux who lived on the Rosebud either noncommittally or in language that reflected then-common white assumptions about cultural differences and the difficulties Indians experienced in adjusting to white ways.

Nevertheless, there might be old people among the Rosebud Sioux who remember the black homesteader with interest or pleasure. Scholar and Sioux expert Herbert T. Hoover recalled a conversation with a tribal elder who referred briefly and pleasantly to a profitable land deal he had made with "a nigger" who used to live in the area.[96] While that individual could have been any of the above-mentioned, Micheaux is certainly a possible candidate for the old Indian's recollection, based on our knowledge of his booster spirit, ready capital, engaging manner, and spirit of entrepreneurship.

Additional research among the oldest generation of Sioux on the Rosebud about Micheaux and other black or mixed-blood settlers could provide new and interesting insights. Obviously, much more work needs to be done among the dusty records and fading memories of early settlers and their descendants if we are truly to understand the breadth and depth of his homesteading experience. This scholar, for one, remains intrigued about aspects of Micheaux's writings that imply more than they reveal.

CHAPTER 5

THE QUEST FOR ROMANCE

The young Oscar Micheaux always assumed that some day a wife would share his life and the homestead empire he intended to build. In practice, her actual acquisition proved to be problematic. For years, he remained intensely idealistic and somewhat priggish about women, strongly believing in the existence "Somewhere" of the "One True Woman". Perhaps he believed he had met her in the person of "the Scottish girl" from the neighboring farm who haunted his writing and films. In seeking a wife, Oscar found himself in the midst of a common social dilemma that required him to choose a mate of his own racial background but placed him in a location where such a choice was impossible. This difficulty was complicated by his necessarily brief visits to the locations where the eligible young women lived. Further, the aspirations of many of these prospective brides did not include frontier drudgery on the godforsaken prairie surrounded by "wild Indians" and white homesteaders.

Probably *The Conquest* is the most accurate chronology of Oscar's search for a wife, although the women he considered appear under different names and in slightly different circumstances in his other books. "Jessie Rooks" makes appearances under several names whenever he writes about making his final choice. Oscar's courtship endeavors were half-hearted until about 1907 when the bittersweet, impossible friendship with "the Scottish girl" made him realize that he needed actively to seek a wife.

The story of this lovely neighbor is sketched in *The Conquest* and expanded in *The Homesteader* and *The Wind From Nowhere*. From these tales, the scholar must attempt to separate fact from legend. Gregory County historians cannot validate the existence of a homestead family with a daughter fitting Micheaux's description. Indeed, that might have been part of Micheaux's intent in writing a disguised autobiography. Harley W. Robinson, Jr., and other family members believe it likely that there was a white woman on the plains who caught his eye and perhaps broke his heart.[97]

All the novels agree on the basic facts: that during the cold, lonely winters in his sod house on the hill he read and wrote. Occasionally he boarded with a neighbor who had a daughter who shared his interests, identified in *The Conquest* only as "the Scottish girl". Proximity blossomed into a friendship that bloomed into an apparently reciprocated love, forcing him to consider his course of action.

In *The Homesteader* and later in *The Wind From Nowhere*, Micheaux voiced his concerns about the perils of over-familiarity with local white girls, some of whom considered him a "good catch". Two passages in *The Wind from Nowhere* are particularly poignant and will sound a familiar note to men of color of a "certain age", who might have been forced by circumstance to walk that precarious chalk line. In this selection, Martin Eden (Micheaux's disguise for this version of his biography) ruminates on his life of lonely popularity.

> ...His white neighbors insisted on kidding him about the girls, all of whom were white, in town and in the neighborhood around him. Yet they were all nice to him.... He almost never heard the ugly word of "nigger", so currently used by white people in referring to one of his race. They seemed to understand that to use it was an insult, and he was surprised to see how much they abstained from using the term.
>
> Every white girl in the country knew him very well and most called him by his first name. They always smiled and engaged him in conversation whenever the opportunity afforded, and were ever solicitous regarding his health. He knew of no place

where he could have had better neighbors and lived so happily. Indeed, he was far more popular, on the whole, than any individual white man. That he was a hard, forward, vigorous worker and was succeeding added to his popularity, and the fact that he was colored seemed to single him out for attention.... Yet with all this, he kept the fact that he was colored well in mind socially and had no thought or intention of misunderstanding the way the white girls treated him. Regardless of how courteous and kind and considerate each was, his interest was limited.

No thought like that of "going with one" entered his mind. He knew that just as soon as he showed signs of transgressing this unspoken rule, he would begin to be confronted with embarrassment. The customs of society had long since decreed that he go his way and they go theirs....[98]

Later, invited to a neighborhood harvest dance, he hesitates before accepting.

...for reasons of his own, he preferred to go alone.   He found the place packed when he got there, with everybody dancing and having a good time.

"Why aren't you dancing, fellow?" everybody seemed to ask him. He made no attempt to do so and made first one excuse and then another, but he mingled with the men and drank beer freely with them. He ate freely, drank more beer, and was really enjoying himself. During the early part of the evening, he glanced across the large floor, and his eyes fell on Deborah [this novel's personification of *The Conquest*'s Scottish girl]... she was looking at him and bowed; he returned the bow. He would have liked to dance, he was fond of it. Deborah wished he'd ask her.

By and by he encountered Ed Vosika, who caught hold of him and [pushed him into a dance with his sister.] ...She waited, looking up at him smiling. He was in a crack.

"Really, I — I don't care to. I — don't know how to dance the way they're dancing out there. I —...."

"Then teach him, Elsie—show him how," cried Ed.

"All right, Mr. Eden," raising her arms. He was in a still deeper crack.

"Please don't, Miss Vosika. Dance with one of the other boys. I'm afraid I'd step on your toes."

"They've been stepped on plenty tonight already," she laughed. "A few more times won't hurt."

At this point, a neighbor happened along, about half intoxicated, and striking him on the shoulder, cried:

"Hello, Eden. Having a good time?"

"Sure, John. Meanwhile, you're a good dancer. Give Miss Vosika a turn."

"Sure thing." He pushed them together and went outside.

He wasn't dancing with any white girl, for everybody to be looking at them. He ran into Bill and George and their father shortly, and they teamed up and had some more beer and some more food. Across the floor, Deborah had seen Eden's action, and thought about him. She began to understand his strange position. She could see now why he had broken down and said that he felt he hadn't a friend in the world. Everybody knew him, everybody liked him. She saw that he was welcome to dance with any of the girls there, including herself, yet he had adroitly avoided doing so. ...in her little life she had never encountered that most ugly of all things, race prejudice. To her, one person was the same as another — all alike. She was so effected [sic] by this that she had no spirit to dance and during the whole affair, she accepted not a single invitation. Just before they were ready to leave for home, she encountered him. She could see that he was slightly intoxicated and she could appreciate why. Maybe he wished to forget some things....[99]

The opposite face of the problem confronted him on his regular visits to black communities in Chicago and New York. Each of the autobiographies, as well as the other novels, dwells at length on the distress felt by many African Americans who worried about cross-racial liaisons. Indeed, in the dialogues between the Micheaux personae and some of the black women, the ladies' palpable rage at the idea of such liaisons reminds late twentieth century readers that black women's resentment of black men's alleged interest in white women is not a new phenomenon.[100]

Social separation was a frequent topic of debate in editorials and general conversation among African Americans everywhere during these years. Black people worried about the fate of the "tragic mulatto" children of such liaisons, citing their difficulty relating to either society. They worried, too, about the temptation for those of fair complexion to "pass" into the white race and disappear, thus depleting the race. And, they worried that cherished cultural values might thus be "bred out of" black life. On the other hand, they worried less about an informal system of color-based hierarchy that was emerging within the race.[101]

Even though these were familiar concerns for many African Americans during this period, the fact that the largest body of Micheaux's work throughout his creative life deals in depth with aspects of miscegenation seems to support the argument that, for this man who had chosen an unfamiliar and lonely path, his discomfort at being caught between two socially incompatible worlds was acute. In Micheaux's "Great Northwest", inter-racial marriages continued to occur among the Indians, although few had taken black spouses. There seem to have been a few black-white marriages in the state that apparently caused little comment; and from Micheaux's description, the family of "the Scottish girl" did not appear to object to a possible match. Like other states, however, South Dakota was in the process of creating an anti-miscegenation law that passed in 1909.[102] Despite his personal pain, Micheaux was forced to return to a belief in the ultimate wisdom of social separation.

In explaining his views, Micheaux wrote negatively about two families in the immediate area who were attempting to "pass" [as white] and expressed his firm conviction that betrayal of one's heritage was not the way to live.[103] While these families seemed to be surviving, and even thriving, he was dubious about the state of their mental health. He knew also that many white people saw through the deception, chuckled or shook their heads, and chose to ignore it. How long this benign neglect would continue was anyone's guess. Jim Crowism was a growing phenomenon throughout the country. During the period immediately after World War I, violent racial incidents would reach alarming proportions throughout the United States.[104] Always, black people in the upper Midwest watched for the unpredictable appearance of southern biases and prejudices among newcomers to the plains, knowing that their intense, outspoken bigotry could fan white uncertainties into full-blown, sometimes tragic incidents from which the Midwest was not immune.

Every black man knew anecdotally, if not through actual experience, that men had been beaten or lynched for far less familiarity than that between Micheaux and the young lady. Micheaux remembered also that Frederick Douglass's late-life second marriage to his white assistant had damaged his credibility with African Americans. Oscar wondered how he could join such a marriage without losing his own credibility among the people of his race whom he hoped to impress and influence by his example of achievement and entrepreneurship. How could he take a lovely young white woman to visit in black Chicago, or to visit his parents now homesteading in central Kansas? The matter of a proper wife had to be solved immediately. Quickly, before the ill-starred romance could progress further, he traveled to Chicago determined to find a black wife.[105]

The Conquest records a procession of possible candidates before Micheaux made his final, ill-fated choice. There was the un-named "octoroon nurse" from St. Louis who

wrote such charming and interesting letters that
for a time they afforded me quite as much entertainment... [as] actual company would have done. In
fact I became so enamoured with her that I nearly
lost my emotional mind, and almost succumbed to
her encouragement toward a marriage proposal. The
death of three of my best horses that fall diverted my
interest; she ceased the epistolary courtship, and I
continued to batch.[106]

There was the strong-minded, plain looking "Daisy Hinshaw"
of Carbondale, "daughter of the most prosperous colored people
in town", but "bold and selfish", demanding that he bring her an
expensive gift, which, unwillingly, he selected for her in a Fifth
Avenue shop in New York City. So presumptious and possessive
was Miss Hinshaw that she dominated his time and ultimately
proposed to him, thus ruining her chance for marriage to him
and driving him back to the arms of gentle Jessie, her best friend.

Jessie's family was now down on its luck, her mail carrier
father having suffered a work-related injury and lost his job. The
family relied on her wages to remain solvent. Nevertheless, she
was soft, loving, and welcoming — a pleasant change from the
demanding Miss Hinshaw. This encounter culminated in a successful engagement and Micheaux returned, heartened, to the
prairie and prepared to receive his bride. Again Jessie's staying
power proved to be limited. Unable to bear their separation, she
succumbed to the attentions of a much-older cook in a local
restaurant and married him, informing the jilted Micheaux after
the fact and severely bruising his pride.[107]

Now it was 1909, and Micheaux's desire for a wife was exacerbated by another circumstance described in detail in *The
Homesteader*. Crops were still excellent and Oscar's harvest of
wheat, flax, and corn had been bountiful. With a little money in
his pocket and excellent credit at the bank, he saw the opportunity to increase his half-section holdings to the 1,000 acres of his
dreams. It was time to purchase Tripp County relinquishments
and the window of opportunity was narrow. He had already

achieved part of his goal by persuading his sister, Olivia, and his grandmother, Melvina, to use their names and his money to file on two parcels of 160 acres each. Now he needed a prospective bride willing to use her maiden name and his money to file on a quarter section before the final deadline.

This called for desperate measures. It was boiling down to a straight business proposition — one that he hoped, of course, would blossom into a great romance. In *The Homesteader* he described how he wrote letters outlining his proposal to three carefully selected black women who might be amenable to such an arrangement. In the letters he portrayed himself as a man of means and prospects, well able to provide a bride with a comfortable life in the "Great Northwest". Circumstances or fate kept the two better choices from responding by Micheaux's deadline.

Orlean McCracken was his third choice. Micheaux disguises her in *The Homesteader* as Orlean McCarthy, in *The Conquest* as Orlean McCraline, and in *The Wind from Nowhere* as Linda Lee. The actual Miss McCracken was the spinster daughter of the African Methodist Church's Presiding Elder for the Southern District of Illinois, N.J. McCracken, formerly the pastor of Micheux's childhood congregation.[108]

All of the accounts agree that Micheaux hardly could have chosen more poorly. Apparently the McCracken family was dysfunctional by almost any standard. Trained as a teacher, Orlean was a shy "daddy's girl" with a manipulative, jealous older sister and a pleasant, brow-beaten mother. The domineering, womanizing father was "king of his castle", bombastic, opinionated, and verbally abusive. Time spent with his mistress of many years, as well as extensive travel required by his job, offered the family respite from his abuse. They also had learned to use deception to survive his tantrums.

Orlean was ill-equipped to leave the security of the city for frontier life and unprepared to cope with her father's displeasure and her sister's jealous manipulations. A pleasant and accommodating girl who survived her sister's domination and ill temper by subordinating herself, Orlean was her father's favorite. To the lascivious, opinionated, and domineering preacher, his daughter was the apple of his eye.

Into this explosive mix walked Oscar Micheaux, a frontier man long accustomed to direct eye-to-eye discourse based on reason. He soon discovered that his uncompromising racial and political views were the antithesis of the Rev. McCracken's. Indeed, the elder represented everything Oscar most disliked about the "Negro race". Not surprisingly, Micheaux alienated his future father-in-law immediately. The Rev. McCracken might have consented to the match only in the belief that his daughter was marrying a wealthy man.

In any event, a chaperoned Miss McCracken made a quick visit to South Dakota prior to the wedding. There she filed on a homestead in Tripp County, not far from the new town of Witten, just before the deadline. The couple then married in Chicago, receiving the following brief notice in the *Chicago Defender* on April 23, 1910:

> Miss Orlean McCracken, daughter of Elder McCracken, was married on Thursday to Mr. Oscar Micheaux of Gregory, S.D. They left the same night on the Golden Gate Limited for their home.[109]

The Gregory *Times Advocate* also reported on Oscar's marriage in a short notation published on April 27, 1910:

> Oscar Micheaux last week quietly slipped away to Chicago where he was married. He and his bride returning [sic] to Gregory Sunday evening. Mr. Micheaux was one of the early homesteaders in this country and owns a half section of land Southeast of town. His bride has a claim in Tripp county and they will make their future home there. The *Times Advocate* joins in wishing this couple a happy journey over life's seas.[110]

After those tantalizing factual wedding announcements, the scholar must return to the fictionalized autobiographies to piece together subsequent events. *The Conquest* reports that on returning to the Rosebud, they quickly set up housekeeping on

Orlean's homestead. This was necessary because of the residence requirement for "proving up". Micheaux had purchased a house in Gregory and arranged to have it moved to the new site. He also moved buildings from the original homestead. These were major logistical undertakings. Not only were there the complexities associated with the physical moving of buildings, a common if complicated practice on the Rosebud, there were distances of 40 to 60 miles involved. Thus, the bride was necessarily left alone during his accomplishment of these essentially masculine tasks.

Oscar's sister, Olivia, and grandmother, Melvina, lived nearby on the homesteads they had acquired with Oscar.[111] Olivia, who had recently married, took the young bride under her wing and did her best to make her feel at home. Orlean, however, was lonely and discontented; unhappy that her groom seemed more involved in the complexities of survival than in paying attention to her. Longtime bachelor Oscar, for his part, seemed to know little about feminine psychology, and felt that he was paying attention to her by ensuring that she would be taken care of in a comfortable house on her own property. An early and unplanned pregnancy compounded the young bride's depression.[112]

The Homesteader and *The Wind From Nowhere* provide additional details that appear to have a factual basis. All three accounts agree that the bride's father and older sister began at once to interfere with the young couple. All agree that Orlean's difficult pregnancy and Oscar's preoccupation with managing five widely separated farmsteads in difficult country with limited liquid cash exacerbated the conflict. All agree that there were a series of escalating confrontations. These were aggravated by the philosophical differences between Micheaux and his father-in-law who shared a concern for Orlean's health; and her father's growing realization that while Micheaux might have the "prospects" of a rich man, he had little liquid capital.

All three accounts describe the birth of a child. In *The Conquest* and *The Homesteader*, it was stillborn. In *The Wind from Nowhere*, the child lived and was later returned to the father. All agree that the birth occurred while Oscar was absent, detained by variously described unavoidable circumstances arising from weather or travel between the homesteads. In

Micheaux's absence, Orlean was attended by a local physician and perhaps by his grandmother and sister; but with complications associated with the delivery, the physician took it upon himself to contact Orlean's father, who arrived on the next train, accompanied by her sister. The three accounts generally agree that the subsequent family altercations were both public and embarrassing, and ended when a weakened Orlean emptied the couple's joint account and allowed herself to be smuggled onto the train for Chicago.[113]

The accounts agree, as will be detailed below, that later, and without Micheaux's consent, the preacher sold the speculative property for much less than its value and kept the money. Repeated attempts, including the threat of legal action by the husband to reclaim his bride and his money, failed, and ultimately the marriage ended in divorce. All three accounts blame Orlean's sister for goading the egotistical and insecure father into final actions that resulted in termination of the marriage.[114]

Scholars generally agree that the separation scene between Orlean and Oscar, which concludes the narrative in *The Conquest*, is factual. Alternative endings found in the remaining autobiographical novels are so heavily fictionalized that it is difficult to determine the presence of any new facts. Indeed, these alternative endings, some quite violent, appear to be cathartic attempts by a deeply wounded man to come to terms with the loss of his marriage. Apparently, no child survived the marriage.

The best evidence that the accounts of the marriage and its untimely end are essentially factual and represent an actual incident in Oscar Micheaux's life is found in a front-page story that appeared in the April 29, 1911, *Chicago Defender*. It compares favorably with the denouement described in *The Conquest*, the most accurate of the autobiographical versions:

MR. OSCAR MICHEAUX IN CITY
Seemed to Be in Family Mix-Up,
Yet Would Not Speak; Seen
With Dr. Daily at Father-in-
Law's door, But Neither He
Nor the Doctor Were Admitted

> Dr. Bryant (White) is Their Family Physician, is Thought Is [sic] the Cause of the Lockout.

– – – – – – –

Seeing Dr. U.G. Daily and Mr. Oscar Micheaux in hot haste turn in Vernon avenue in the 3200 block, our reporter took out after them but remained a block behind to see what was the cause. But [by] the time he got up to the door of Rev. N.J. McCracken, the two gentlemen were standing waiting for the door to be opened, but after our reporter got to the corner of 32d street and Vernon avenue and stood for about half an hour waiting to see what was to be pulled off, the two gentlemen descended the steps and proceeded up the street, Mr. Micheaux gesticulating with both hands to the doctor. Our reporter then became interested. Half an hour later he went to the Keystone hotel where Mr. Micheaux was stopping, and tried to interview him, but he evaded our reporter. He knew they were after him, leaving his keys at the office to make it appear that he was out, but this did not stop our reporter, for he saw him go in, so he went up to the parlor, found the gentleman seated reading the Defender.

Our reporter struck up a conversation about his 1,000 acres of land in South Dakota and then ask[ed] about the father-in-law's trip out to his home which he admitted he was out there and had a pleasant stay, also admitted his wife returned with her father, but says she came to spend the summer for she was quite sick. When asked why he was not admitted with Dr. Daily he said he thought they were downtown at the time, but we do know that Mr. Micheaux has only seen his wife once during his week's stay in the city.

Before he left on Wednesday our reporter saw
him in a telephone booth trying to get the number,
but he did not seem to stay on the line; he got his
party and they rang off; he left the city on the 5:20
train the same afternoon and when our reporter
tried to get to see him he locked himself in his drawing room and would not see anyone.

He is the only colored farmer in his country
[county?] and stands well with the business world of
that section, so much so that the United States government has appointed him to an office for that section of the state. He is worth $150,000, all told.[115]

The description of the phone call matches Micheaux's
accounts of his effort to reconcile with his wife through the intervention of the minister's long-time paramour.[116]

Back home on the Rosebud, Micheaux was distraught over
the rift in his marriage and enraged at his father-in-law. Still, he
had every reason to expect, that spring of 1911, that his financial
future in agriculture remained bright. In his six years of homesteading in Gregory and Tripp counties, he had prospered. He
was personally farming 410 acres and had rented another 110 to
another farmer. His crop yields had generally been fair to good,
although 1910 had seemed a little dry. Still, land values had continued to rise, and he saw no reason why that should not continue.[117] Unbeknownst to him, however, the treacherous Great
Plains was about to test the mettle of its most recent settlers.

Spring came early that year and was unusually warm and dry.
In May, he noted with some concern that a field of spelt had lost
some of its springtime freshness, and the soil around it seemed
dry although it had recently rained.[118] The weather cycle had
come full circle, just as the Indians and old timers knew it would.
Other more recent immigrants, especially those from the steppes
of Russia, were not surprised. Sometime in the midst of
Micheaux's domestic travail, he had become acquainted with a
pair of German-Russian brothers, part of the forced immigration
from Russia aimed primarily at German Mennonites who were no

longer welcome in a rapidly modernizing Russia. John and Jacob Wesinberger (which might not have been their correct names) owned homesteads in Mellette County [north of Tripp County] and "owned 150 head of cattle, 75 head of horses, hogs, and all kinds of farm machinery, besides a steam prairie breaking outfit and 1500 acres of land between them".[119] Often Micheaux visited them, swapped yarns, and was intrigued by their interest in astronomy and meteorology. The brothers shared with him the European folk belief that weather cycles could be predicted by the study of astronomy, and provided anecdotal data that appeared to support this belief.

"Jupiter," said John, as he leisurely rolled a ciga-
rette, "circumnavigates the sun once while the earth
goes around it twelve times. In Russia [when]
Jupiter's position got between the sun and the constellations Pisces, Aries, Taurus, and Gemini, it was
invariably wet and cool and small grain crops were
good, but as it passed on and got between the sun
and the constellations Libra and Scorpio it was
always followed by a minimum of rainfall and a
maximum heat, which caused a severe drouth [sic]."
They had hoped it would be different in America,
but explained further that when they had lived in
Russia, it commenced to get dry around St.
Petersburg, Warsaw, and all northern Russia a year
or so before it did in southern Russia. They had relatives living around Menno, in Hutchinson County,
South Dakota, who had witnessed the disastrous
drouth [sic] during Cleveland's administration.
Jupiter was nearing the position it had then occupied and would, in sixty days, be at the same position it had been at that time.... I did a little thinking
and remembered it had been dry in southern Illinois
at the time and I began to feel somewhat
uneasy....[120]

Whether the brothers' folk knowledge was scientifically based or not, it proved remarkably accurate. The drought, which had quietly begun the previous year, soon made its presence felt with a vengeance across the central United States. Newspapers reported that crops in Oklahoma and Kansas were scorched beyond salvation. From Kansas City to the Colorado line, it was a grim time for farmers. Settlers all over the upper midwest, who had ridden the land boom in high optimism, began to desert their claims and farms, in a forlorn procession of worn out, discourged people and animals. Micheaux heard that at Pierre 700 wagons crossed the Missouri River in a single day, headed east, and on a trip to visit friends seventeen miles away, he passed forty-seven houses, only one of which was occupied.[121]

The economy in the Rosebud's boom towns was collapsing. Merchants were being pressed by the wholesale houses to settle their bills. Townspeople and farmers who had spent lavishly on the newfangled automobiles found themselves in default. Speculators who had bet their last dollar on mortgages they could no longer afford were unable to find buyers. Tripp County was especially hard hit because it had opened at the peak of the boom, and the unusual prosperity had caused people to become reckless. New settlers who had not paid the government's price of $6 an acre and had bought at inflated rates of $25-45 per acre could find no one willing to meet their price.

The land was hot, dry, and windy. Dead vegetation gave way to dust. Long, hot days were broken briefly by brief and terrible thunder storms that appeared in scattered and unpredictable locations, drenching, but not quenching, the parched earth and temporarily filling draws and ravines to overflowing, selectively saving some of the crops.

Desperate to save his crops and husband his rapidly diminishing capital, Micheaux harvested what he could. His wheat threshed at about eight hundred bushels. At market, it did not bring enough to make expenses. Another trip to Chicago to try to save his marriage was impossible, and because he knew Orlean shared his letters with her family, he was reluctant to admit to them that he was in trouble. Besides, infrequent communication with the Elder and others close to the family made it clear that a trip would be wasted effort.

All during that long year Micheaux wrestled with his problems. Over-extended and facing foreclosure, he knew that personal bankruptcy was a real possibility. Salvation depended on the return of the seasonal rain and snow, or on some unsuspected source of income.[122]

Then, when matters could get no worse, they did. A local banker with no love for Micheaux knew that the gullible Elder McCracken had no idea of the value of his daughter's homestead, which had been purchased with Micheaux's money. He prevailed upon the Chicago preacher to sell the quarter section for only $300. McCracken made certain that Micheaux never saw any of the money. Furious, Oscar made one final trip to Chicago and through a series of devious maneuvers managed to see Orlean alone for the last time. The visit was aborted by the unexpected appearance of Elder McCracken, who forced Orlean to choose between her husband and her father.[123] That was the end of the marriage.

Back home, Micheaux unsuccessfully pursued legal action to try to recover some of his investment money and salvage what he could of his farmstead ventures. The most pressing need was financial. What could he do? How could he raise some quick cash? Perhaps he could write a book. It would pass the time and serve as a catharsis. There was always the chance that someone might publish it in time to rescue him from financial ruin.

With that decision, Micheaux embarked upon the next phase of his career.

CHAPTER 6
THE WRITER

Before he could begin writing his "best seller", Oscar needed to attend to his farming, buy some time, and try to avoid following his neighbors into bankruptcy. During those terrible days when many over-confident settlers faced foreclosure and bankruptcy after three years of crop failures, Micheaux's financial problems caused no particular comment, but he fought against feelings of personal disgrace. South Dakota's state law provided a measure of respite for hard-pressed owners by allowing redemption of foreclosed property within one year from the foreclosure date or, alternatively, the option of paying the interest and taxes, which allowed an additional year to redeem the land. Although he faced the loss of his land investments through both foreclosure and title disputes, he was not a man to give up easily. He paid the interest and taxes. There was enough wheat seed left from his meager harvest to plant one crop, and this he did while ruminating on the story he planned to write as soon as the planting was finished.

With the crop in the ground, he sat down to write his first book which he titled *The Conquest: The Story of a Negro Pioneer*. Later, in his second book, *The Homesteader*, he chronicled his experience with this frustrating process. Micheaux, as the hard-pressed protagonist, Jean Baptiste, reasoned that since, in his humble opinion, he was a prolific and practical thinker as well as a great reader, it naturally followed that he could teach himself to write:

> Of writing he knew little and the art of composition appeared very difficult. But of thought, this he

had a-plenty. Well, after all, that was the most essential. If one has thoughts to express, it is possible to
learn very soon some method of construction. So
after some weeks of speculation, he bought himself
a tablet, some pencils and took up the art of writing.

He found no difficulty in saying something. The
first day he wrote ten thousand words. The next day
he reversed the tablet and wrote ten thousand more.
In the next two days he re-wrote the twenty thousand, and on the fifth day he tore it into shreds and
threw it to the winds....[124]

Eventually a story took shape as Oscar poured out his frustration in a disguised autobiography about a thwarted marriage,
the father-in-law whom he portrayed as the personification of
evil, and an engrossing and remarkably accurate tale about the
settling of the Rosebud. Untrained as a writer, with the novice's
lack of knowledge about techniques of plot and planning, he
wrote from instinct, consumed by his story. In *The Homesteader*
he pinpointed accurately one of the technical problems that critics would agree plagued him throughout his writing career:

Through the beautiful, windy autumn days, he
labored at his difficult task, the task of telling a story.
The greatest difficulty he encountered was that he
thought faster than he could write.
Therefore he often broke off right in the middle
of a sentence to relate an incident that would occur
to him to tell of something else.[125]

When he had completed a first draft, Oscar took the manuscript to a sympathetic friend whose interest evaporated quickly
when he saw the stack of tablets. Meanwhile, news that the "colored homesteader" was writing a book circulated, and his neighbors became interested and curious. Many shared his desperate
plight and hoped that a "patriotic boosting of the country through
a book" would be an effective and subtle way to advertise the

area and perhaps help them recoup their rapidly escalating losses. Eventually he found a local lawyer who agreed to help him
correct and edit the work for a price.[126] On the Rosebud, the
story lingers that Micheaux's benefactor had great difficulty collecting his fee (in hindsight forgetting, perhaps, that many
Rosebud obligations went by the wayside during those years). A
woman in nearby Dixon typed the corrected version and helped
him refine the story, and Oscar began the discouraging process
of attempting to interest a publisher.

On December 12, 1912, the *Dallas News* published an item
that suggests Micheaux's work was being favorably considered
for publication in the *Saturday Evening Post*:

> The Rosebud Country has always been able to
> boast of the majority of doings but the opportunity
> is now afforded to add on more to the list. A real
> author who is recognized. Some months ago Oscar
> Micheaux, one of the old citizens of the Rosebud
> Country concluded that the Rosebud should be
> given a proper historical write-up from the stand-
> point of one who had farmed and one who had
> assisted in the development of this vast prairie from
> its grass stage until today with its $75 land [and] $100
> land with its railroad facilities and telephone con-
> nections. This conclusion reached, he has proposed
> the same for publication and presented [it] to the
> Saturday Evening Post, for a serial story. The editors
> of the publication are now re-editing the works, and
> it is expected soon that the same will be in print.
> The McClury Publishing Company will print the
> same in book form is the information given us from
> a reliable source. Oscar, accept our congratulations.
> We know that your story will be interesting and will
> assist in the efforts are making to boost the
> Rosebud and tell the world of her unqualified
> advantages.[127]

A careful search of *Saturday Evening Post* archives for the period in question has failed to turn up any evidence that Micheaux's story was actually published. In *The Homesteader*, he spoke of receiving a series of rejections, and eventually giving up hope of ever interesting an eastern publisher in the personal homesteading story of a black writer.

He tried writing short stories but they fared no better and he eventually decided it was a waste of postage to send them out for consideration. Finally, an acquaintance informed him that one could self-publish and self-market a book. Immediately, he investigated how this might be done. In the words of *Homesteader* protagonist Jean Baptiste, he told of securing the name and address of a company that would manufacture a book of more than 300 pages for fifty cents per copy. In his impecunious state, this seemed a great deal of money, but he resolved to make the effort. His circumstances were desperate. Micheaux had no money, nor did he have a suit of clothes appropriate for a visit to a publisher.

With everything to gain and nothing to lose, Oscar decided to draw on his sales knowledge and let his neighbors know that there really was going to be a book about the Rosebud. On March 20, 1913, he wrote to the Gregory *Times Advocate*.

> The Times Advocate is in receipt of a letter from Oscar Micheaux giving notice of a book which he had written and will soon be issued by the publishers. The book is entitled "The Conquest" and is a novel story of the development of the Rosebud Country. Mr. Micheaux has spent several years in the country and is well versed in the early history and progress, and there is no doubt as to the interest the publication will have for readers in the famous Rosebud country. The Publishers commend the work to the reading public and speak of it as a very interesting history of the frontier life.[128]

The Jackson brothers, now operating their bank at at the relocated town of Dallas, were Micheaux's only possible source of temporary funds for travel to the publisher, but it was fifty miles from his homestead in Tripp County to their offices. Borrowing $5.00 from his local banker, he made his way to Dallas where he laid problem and proposition on the desk of banker Graydon Jackson, who loaned him fifty dollars to make the trip. At the clothiers across the street, he purchased a new suit, charging the outfit to his account.

Two days later he presented himself and his manuscript at the printer in Lincoln, Nebraska. Company officials registered surprise at meeting an "Ethiopian" but, after several days of negotiation, they agreed to manufacture 1,000 copies at 75 cents a copy based on receipt of $250 before going to press.[129]

He had concluded his deal just in time. On April 3, 1913, a notice of foreclosure appeared in the local press. In the same issue of the paper was the following story:

> Oscar Micheaux of Witten was in the city Saturday taking orders for his book, "The Conquest." He says he is meeting with great success and already has enough orders to ensure the publication of the book. The editor had the opportunity to read the first chapter of the book and can heartily recommend it as an interesting story if the first chapter is any criteria.[130]

Recounting the experience in *The Homesteader*, Micheaux recalled that he returned home with a prospectus which he used to canvass settlers in Gregory and Tripp counties, offering them an opportunity to buy his book about life on the Rosebud.[131] His neighbors recognized that Oscar's book was about their lives as well as his own and apparently were eager to purchase copies of the fully-illustrated volume, which sold for $1.50 a copy.[132] The *Times Advocate* continued to boost sales by regular coverage:

> May 8, 1913. Oscar Micheaux was in town yesterday delivering a few advance copies of the novel entitled "The Conquest, A Story of the Rosebud." The book has had a wonderful sale and is pro-

nounced by those who have read it as being an
excellent story.[133]

To be sure, Micheaux's early years as a produce peddler in
the Illinois farmers' market stood him in good stead, for he
declared that within two weeks he had secured orders for 1500
copies. When he received his first shipment of *The Conquest: The
Story of a Negro Homesteader*, he delivered his orders and paid
the printer. There was enough left, he said, to deposit $2500 "to
the credit of the book in the bank".[134] Obviously, the sale of his
book offered the best hope for his continued financial health.

Records show that *The Conquest* was first published in 1913
by Woodruff Press of Lincoln, Nebraska, and appeared without
mention of the author. Micheaux never explained why he chose
to publish anonymously, but there are clues. James Weldon
Johnson's *Autobiography of an Ex-Colored Man* had appeared
without attribution the previous year and was enjoying modest
sales among African Americans. Micheaux might have been
intrigued by that concept. He might also have been believed that
writing anonymously lessened his liability. There was always the
potential for confrontation or legal action by the McCrackens,
and his sharp criticism of Rosebud locals might also have occasioned action for libel. Another clue appears in his second book,
The Forged Note, wherein protagonist Sidney Wyeth, coincident-
ly a "colored" South Dakota homesteader, was peddling his own
book under the title of *The Tempest: The Story of a Negro Pioneer*,
also published without attribution. In that case, "Wyeth"
explained to his agents that identifying himself as the author of a
book he was trying to sell would diminish its value.[135] Later editions of *The Conquest* carried his by-line.

After his early success with local sales, Micheaux's next problem was to set up a practical distribution system that would reach
African Americans throughout the country. He wanted his book
to proclaim to the race what he had learned about getting ahead
in a white man's world, and make them aware of the boundless
opportunities that remained even in the drought-ravaged "Great
Northwest". Through the book he would vindicate his life, stand

as an inspiration for his people, and have the last laugh on his nemesis, Elder N.J. McCracken.

Oscar tried first to place *The Conquest* with established black traveling agents who peddled a variety of goods in African American rural and urban neighborhoods, "especially hair goods to make their curls grow or hang straighter, — or in complexion creams to clarify and whiten the skin".[136] He soon discovered that shipping logistics and the commission expectations of the less-than-enthusiastic salesmen made this system impractical. Undaunted, he decided to sell it himself and hire his own agents to handle his books exclusively through door-to-door commission sales in black communities.

Because he had built his land acquisitions by mortgaging his homesteads, he faced foreclosure on nearly all of them. Orlean's property was gone for a pittance that had enriched her father, and the subsequent divorce had ended the matter legally if not morally. Local evidence suggests that Micheaux was not willing to let the matter drop. Apparently, he had decided to take legal action against his former father-in-law.

By July, 1913, many of his neighbors had read *The Conquest: The Story of a Negro Pioneer* and had learned his version of the details of his marital debacle. In an isolated rural area with few diversions, tales of the Micheauxs' troubled marriage must have been grist for the local gossip mill. Perhaps it was this gossip that resulted in the single negative local newspaper article that has been uncovered about Oscar Micheaux. Interestingly, it is the only local article uncovered to date that identifies him as a Negro. Dated July 31, 1913, and headlined "Oscar Micheaux Starts Damage Suit", the article continues:

> Oscar Micheaux, the Negro Author of the recent book purporting to describe life on the Rosebud Reservation and entitled "The Conquest" announced that he has instituted a suit for $10,000 damages against his father-in-law for alienating his wife's affections. The defendant in the action is a prominent minister in Chicago. The trial of the case will bring forth some interesting evidence it is alleged.[137]

The lawsuit might not have gone far; if it did, there is no evidence that it was successful, perhaps because the minister's financial resources were limited. It is difficult to get blood out of a turnip. Gradually, Micheaux lost all of the homesteads to foreclosure except the one his sister, Olivia, had left him when she and her husband returned to Kansas. There was little to lose by gambling on a career as a writer, and already he had an idea for a second book.

Apparently, he wrote his second book, *The Forged Note*, while nominally living on the Rosebud and traveling intermittently to set up the distribution network that would culminate in the establishment of his own publishing house in Sioux City, Iowa. *The Forged Note* relates in detail how his distribution system worked and how he hired and managed his agents.[138] Describing sales trips into the heart of the Deep South, it records his culture shock at a plunge into black Atlanta (Attalia), black Birmingham (Effingham), and black New Orleans. He was appalled at how discouragingly different, impoverished, and hopelessly backward African Americans in those great cities seemed compared to those in Chicago, Cincinnati, New York, and the Midwest.

In *The Forged Note*, which seems to have been a conscious attempt at the novel form, Micheaux, in the guise of protagonist Sidney Wyeth, a former South Dakota homesteader, tours major cities in the Midwest and South to sell his book, *The Tempest: The Story of a Negro Pioneer*. In each city he hires and trains agents to peddle it door to door. Throughout the book, the convoluted story line returns to the theme of Wyeth's search for the "One True Woman" in the mutual and star-crossed attraction between his protagonist and Mildred Latham, a lovely lady with a mysterious past.

Along the way, sub-themes appear, featuring interesting and evocative encounters with various engaging ghetto personalities who speak in dialect or an early version of "hipster" slang. These themes graphically depict the debilitating poverty and the seamier sides of southern ghetto life and show the harsh realities of black survival in the South during a precarious time for the race.

Wyeth, Oscar Devereaux, and Jean Baptiste are Micheaux's three main fictionalized autobiographical personalities, supplemented later in his films by others possessing similar qualities. These heroes consistently appear as educated, assimilated men who speak standard English and uphold middle-class values and morality while retaining a strong race pride. They believe deeply in African Americans' ability to pull themselves up by their bootstraps if they will only apply themselves. Others characters who reflect these values and lifestyles always include at least one heroine and a few key families or individuals. All of them freely expound their middle-class theories and air their prejudices about why the black masses are having such difficulty improving their lot. Also, these characters are contemptuous of the class of quasi-aristocrats that black sociologist E. Franklin Frazier would later characterize as the "black bourgeoisie". Frazier's term referred to a segment of society usually distinguished by fair complexion who projected a shallow veneer of education and upper class ambitions that camouflaged inferior education and professional training and a conspicuous lack of curiosity about any matters that would mark them as truly "cultivated".[139] For Micheaux, the group included teachers and college professors, physicians and, not unexpectedly, most of the clergy.

Many of the concerns and criticisms of African Americans' lack of progress that Micheaux expresses through his protagonists were shared and expressed by the black social engineers and academicians who conceived and publicized the concept of the Harlem Renaissance from which Micheaux was pointedly excluded. It was not until the depression of the 1930s destroyed the cultural progress of the few, including independent entrepreneurs like Micheaux, that the black leadership was able to come fully to grips with the economic and social effects of the white economic and political stranglehold which formed the basis of American racism.[140]

Predictably, the "black bourgeoisie" annoyed Oscar because of their apparent lack of interest in furthering their education and increasing their knowledge through reading and, by extension, through buying his books. He was appalled to find that virtually no black businesses in large southern communities stocked magazines, periodicals, or books by black authors on the grounds that there was no market for them. There was more interest in establishing parks and a colored YMCA than in building libraries. Maids working for white families, who met the salesmen at the employer's kitchen door and placed orders that they invariably honored with payment, became Micheaux's best customers.[141]

The Forged Note explores other aspects of Jim Crowism and southern repression. In a memorable chapter, Wyeth and one of his new hipster acquaintances decide to spend an evening "answering the call of the wild", as Micheaux had often done without question on the Rosebud. Emerging from a tavern in the ghetto during the early hours of the morning, slightly the worse for wear, they are arrested by a pair of stereotypical bigoted policemen, irritated at encountering an "uppity nigger" who asserts that it is his right to be on the street whenever he chooses. A night in jail and an expensive experience with white injustice before a corrupt judge who refuses to expunge the record and threatens to continue to drain his pocketbook finishes Wyeth's experience with Attalia (Atlanta). Leaving one of his agents in charge, he moves his base of operations to Effingham (Birmingham).[142]

Like the other autobiographies, *The Forged Note* continues Micheaux's battle with the black clergy. Protagonist Wyeth's "One True Woman" is Mildred Latham, a Cincinnati native, perhaps modeled after a more mature version of Orlean, whose corrupt preacher father had embezzled money to purchase a bishopric for himself. To protect her father, she becames the mistress of the white man who had saved him, escaping from this fate only at the man's death, when she receives a large inheritance as compensation.

Mildred enters Wyeth's life after becoming an agent for his book but, believing her to be a "soiled dove", he distances himself from her. Always fearful that her damaged reputation will follow her, she moves restlessly from city to city, finally seeking refuge in Memphis where she finds lodgings with an honorable bachelor clergyman and his spinster sister. While rooming with them, she learns that the pastor is obsessed with the need to build a YMCA for local African Americans. A northern philanthropist has offered a donation, contingent on matching funds from the impoverished black community. With a renewed threat of exposure facing her in Memphis, Mildred flees again, but not before anonymously leaving her considerable inheritance to her host for the YMCA fund drive.

Eventually, Wyeth and Mildred meet again in New Orleans when, as his most productive sales agent, she saves his book business while he is hospitalized near death from typhoid. This time, true love runs smoothly. The reader is left to imagine that they will marry and return to the haven of the Rosebud. This implied ending might have caused Micheaux problems years later when he resurrected an unmarried Sidney Wyeth in a mystery story, which deals with his courtship and marriage to a beautiful mixed-race German immigrant woman.

The YMCA episode is an example of Micheaux's use of contemporary events in black America to further a story. White Americans had imported the Young Men's Christian Association from England in 1858 as a rigidly segregated institution aimed at managing urban immigrants. In the early teens, white philanthropists, including Sears Roebuck tycoon, Julius Rosenwald, offered substantial matching funds for black leaders to construct segregated Y's in urban neighborhoods. Issues of the 1909-1911 *Chicago Defender* carried regular coverage on that community's campaign to fund and build its own "colored" YMCA.[143]

Modern critic Randal Woodland described *The Forged Note* as one that demonstrates the author's increased skill in telling a good story while providing "an inspirational example for others of his race by positing that success comes to the diligent. He intended to criticize those members of the race, be they gamblers or Baptist preachers, who were not contributing to the general welfare".[144]

Not surprisingly, the book garnered mixed reviews both for his controversial views and his skill as a writer. During the teens, few "Afro-American" authors were writing novels that met the exacting standards of critics, black or white. White publishing houses were reluctant to risk printing any works by black writers and, when they did, made little attempt to boost sales. James Weldon Johnson's *Autobiography of an Ex-Colored Man* had appeared anonymously in 1912. Although it was read in African American circles, it was not known widely until Knopf rescued and re-issued it in 1927 as a result of Johnson's leadership in the NAACP and the Harlem Renaissance. During the teens, Paul Lawrence Dunbar and Charles Chestnutt were the two best known black writers. While critics considered some of their work "good", much of it received the same criticism from both races that Micheaux's work faced. Many African American leaders felt strongly that nothing should appear in print to provide white racists with more negative ammunition. They were stung by Micheaux's criticism of black life, although the scenes he described commonly appeared in black newspapers of the day.

While his self-marketing ability saved him from the economic impact of this criticism, it deprived him of the constructive benefit of access to a competent editor. Nonetheless, he gained a measure of financial independence and built a lasting, nationwide core of loyal readers who often agreed with his personal philosophy while enjoying a good melodrama.

Perhaps as early as 1914 and continuing until he began making his first film in 1918, Micheaux divided his time between the Rosebud, Lincoln, Nebraska, Sioux City, Iowa, and travel throughout the South and Midwest to peddle his books. On the Rosebud during World War I, after losing his own property to foreclosure, he apparently rented a house on the Ed LaPour farm near Gregory, normally occupied by LaPour's brother, then serving in the military.[145]

In Lincoln, Micheaux published *The Forged Note* in 1915 with Woodruff Printers under his own publishing imprint, which he later moved to Sioux City. He called his firm The Western Book and Supply Company and it appeared in various guises throughout his business career. By the fall of 1915 he was back on the Rosebud peddling his second book, and apparently Rosebud public opinion had swung again in his favor:

> September 15, 1915. Oscar Micheaux, who filed
> on a homestead in Gregory County in the early 90s
> [sic] and is well known both in Gregory and Tripp
> Counties is in Colome this week taking orders for a

new book entitled "The Forged Note." He says he is
meeting with splendid success. He is one of the
most ambitious colored men we ever met and he is
bound to succeed. He gained considerable fame a
few years ago when he wrote and published his
book, "The Conquest" which dealt with local characters and conditions. - *Colome Times*[146]

Local historians suggest that the move to Sioux City, historically the site of a small, stable, African American community,
might have been prompted by the presence there of a strong and
tolerant community of Jewish businessmen who could be helpful
to the young black entrepreneur.[147] Indeed, during his residence
the town boasted no fewer than five synagogues.

Incorporated in 1857 as a frontier post on the Missouri River
to service steamboat trade to forts and settlements along the
upper reaches of the river, Sioux City, Iowa, was located at the
confluence of the Missouri and the Big Sioux rivers and had
experienced healthy growth. Then, as now, it prided itself on its
diversity. It had become an established trade center and was the
largest and closest city to the up-river settlements. By 1915, it
boasted a population of 61,787 and was a hub for six railroad systems with 18 lines and more than 100 passenger trains arriving
and departing daily. Two major midwestern lines, the Great
Northern and the Chicago, Milwaukee and St. Paul, had located
their railroad shops in the town.[148] Brick and tile works, outfitting
companies for homesteaders and local farmers, more than 100
wholesale and jobbing houses, banks, and an active Board of
Trade provided ample opportunities for both skilled and
unskilled work for people of all races.[149]

Polk's City Directories provide the most accessible clues to
Micheaux's experience in Sioux City. Like census records, Polk's
Directories, published for many American cities from the earliest
years, can be important sources for locating individuals, but
whether a resident appeared in the directory for a given year
depended on his willingness to be listed and on whether he or a
neighbor happened to be available when the enumerator came
calling. Directories not only listed businesses and their owners,

but also residents by address, the spouse's name in parentheses, the head of household's occupation, and whether they were rooming or boarding at the address. Some early directories are especially valuable to scholars seeking African Americans because black people were delineated by the letter "c" (colored) after the name.

Located only about 150 miles from the Rosebud, bustling Sioux City, with its eclectic mix of people and its more than 500 African American residents, must have provided Micheaux with a welcome respite from the isolation and racial homogeneity of the plains. Although he might have resided intermittently in the city as early as 1914, he apparently was enumerated only twice, in 1917 and 1918. These two directories provide incontrovertible proof of his residence, and an examination of the volumes themselves provides evocative insights into the mileau of his busy multi-cultural working class neighborhood. The 1917 Directory lists the author on page 333:

"Micheaux, Oscar (c), trav. agent, rms. 717 W. 6th."[150]

The designation "trav. agent" was the common abbreviation for traveling salesmen or sales representatives. This address was occupied by at least four other individuals:

"J.D. Anthony (c) (Maude), attendant West Hotel
Bath Room, r. 717 W. 6th"
"Mrs. Alice Dalhay (c) r. 717 W. 6th"
"Gustav Dalhay (c) r. 717 W. 6th"[151]

The house has long since disappeared leaving only a grassy vacant lot.

West Sioux City is a unique neighborhood that retains its early flavor despite urban renewal projects that removed the most dilapidated buildings during the 1960s and replaced them with parks and well-kept low income housing. Bounded on the south by the Missouri River, on the west by Hamilton Boulevard adjacent to the Big Sioux River bluffs, and on the east by Grandview Boulevard, the triangle-shaped community adjoins the primary, more prestigious downtown business district on the east and begins where 6th and 7th Streets make abrupt turns north to form West Sioux City's business community.

Here, before 1920, dwelt a melting pot of African Americans and working class whites both native born and immigrant, amidst assorted family businesses, livery stables, and light industry. Micheaux chose rooms located conveniently near the business district. With just a few minutes walk to 7th Street, he could find nearly anything he needed or desired.

For example, at #223 7th Street, Romie DeHart (c) operated a restaurant in 1917.

Dr. R.A. Dobson was a physician, perhaps of African American descent, who practiced medicine at #400.[152] At #404, F.A. Hackley (c) cut hair. Down the street at #413 L.F. Sadler (c) ran a billiard parlor; and at #418, next to Sioux City Hose Company #2, Mrs. Anna Bramer (c) lived and operated a restaurant.

Like all such neighborhoods, many residents were transient. In 1917 at #614 G.C. Carr (c) cut hair and at #704 C.F. Williams (c) advertised his services as a carpet cleaner. Both were gone in 1918. At #806, A.E. Williams (c) was a carpet weaver in 1917 but had moved by the next year.

Interspersed with these African American businesses and residences were white owned businesses with names ranging from C.C. White, who ran a grocery store at #207, to F.M. Kennard's Coal and Feed at #216, to Kazos and Karroc's Restaurant at #321 and Henry Zeckman's Pool Hall at #323. At #450, Isaac Magilevsky ran a grocery store; and Benjamin Cohen sold clothing at #424. C.R. Strauss operated the drugstore at #401 just down the street from the Palace Theatre, Louis Nartz's Bakery, and Allensworth's Meats. H.B. Hawley and Thomas Ward covered the neighborhood second hand market. In the 500 block one could find the Sioux City Wire and Iron Works, L.V. Hegron's Hardware Store, the Bismarck Hotel, and F.E. Peaker, Printer.

Mount Zion Baptist Church and Malone African Methodist Church with combined memberships totaling nearly 200, served the black community.[153] Both were in easy walking distance of Micheaux's lodgings, but given his lack of appreciation for the church during this period of his life, he probably did not attend often. Some of Sioux City's black men might also have belonged to the Decatur Lodge. It met at 417 Douglas and its officers included Worthy Master Mansfield Askew.[154] Askew had come to Sioux City in 1895 from Yankton, South Dakota, looking for work. He was still active in local African American affairs in the early 1960s.[155] If Micheaux was selling *The Conquest* and *The Forged Note* in Sioux City, the men's club might have provided a ready source of customers, since the some of the books' descriptions would have mirrored experiences of black Iowans or immigrants from the south.

Unlike many northern cities with their ethnic or racial neighborhoods, this community appears to have been well integrated. African American families lived in homes next to white families in neighborhoods covering many blocks. Many of the black families owned their own homes. They held jobs ranging from laborer to mail carrier. They worked as club or hotel attendants, domestics and yard men for wealthy citizens, or as porters for businesses or on the railroad. Their white neighbors' names reflected an American melting pot from nearly every European country.

The 1918 Polk's City Directory's entry for Micheaux raises more questions than it answers and will provide scholars with yet additional opportunities for speculation and additional research. On page 334 the entry reads:

> "Micheaux, Oscar (c) (Sarah), author.
> rms 412 1/2 W. 6th."[156]

This entry is interesting for two reasons. Micheaux now felt comfortable identifying himself as an author. More tantalizing, however, is the presence of "Sarah," who apparently shared his rooms at a time when he was believed to have been a bachelor. A glance at his immediate family appears to rule out Sarah as a female relative. The dedication to his sisters in *The Wind from Nowhere* published in 1941 lists them by name:

To My Sisters: Ida, Maude, Olivia, Ethel, and Gertrude
and to Veatrice, who is dead.[157]

His mother was Belle and his grandmother was Melvina.
Several scenarios suggest themselves. One might be based on
a clue in the lengthy dedication of the first edition of *The Forged
Note* (1915). Addressed "To One Whose Name Does Not Appear",
it reads in part,

> I am leaving you and Dixie land tomorrow. It is
> customary, perhaps to say, "Dear Old Dixie," but,
> since I happen to be from that little place off in the
> northwest, of which I have fondly told you, the
> Rosebud Country, where I am returning at once, and
> which is the only place that is dear to me, I could
> not conscientiously use the other term.... When I
> come back it will not be for "color"; [sic] but—well,
> I guess you know. New Orleans, La., August 1, 1915.
> O.M.[158]

Could Sarah have been the mystery person to whom this
book was dedicated? Perhaps he met her in Louisiana and she
joined him in Sioux City in time for the 1918 enumeration. This
scenario argues for Sarah as a person of African American
descent.

A second scenario could devolve around the possibility that
the "Scottish girl" or some other lady friend from the Rosebud
might have managed to join him briefly in Sioux City. Even in a
city as small as Sioux City, inter-racial couples were not
unknown, and as long as they conducted themselves with dis-
cretion would not have been harassed in the mostly live-and-let-
live atmosphere of West Sioux City. The spouse's race does not
appear in the Directories, so its absence in the case of Sarah
proves nothing.

Who was Sarah? Did her presence mean that his broken heart
was mending?

Perhaps, like the woman who appeared in *The Forged Note*,
she only helped him in his business, handling orders and main-

taining stock while he traveled and sold the three titles that made up his early work. And perhaps that is what the prim and proper author wanted his public to believe if her presence later came to light. Or, perhaps they were married and the marriage did not endure. The facts are virtually impossible to reconstruct. Access to contemporary black newspapers might offer clues, but many issues have been lost. The respected *Sioux City Journal* devoted little space to "negroes", except on issues of law and order. Micheaux, climbing to his goal of role model for the race, would have understood the value of keeping his private life private. Quite possibly this single insert in the Polk's Directory of 1918 will remain the only clue to the real Micheaux living beneath his carefully constructed personal biography.

His 1918 address in the 400 block of West Sixth Street did not exist in 1917. In 1918 it was home to a new business known as L.P. Wycoff, Auto Painting. Apparently Micheaux and Sarah occupied the only apartment, which was located either upstairs or at the rear of the lot.[159] Their landlord was a prominent local businessman, Lawton P. Wycoff, who, according to the 1917 Polk's Directory, operated a business located at 1627 Douglas as "Cord-Wycoff Tire and Rubber Company" that sold autos and auto supplies, and at 408 5th Street, where he dealt in real estate.[160] Judging by his 1918 expansion, Mr. Wycoff seemed to be finding the new automobile a prosperous source of income. Like the first address, the building is long gone, replaced by a grassy vacant lot across from a new park.[161]

Micheaux would have found Sioux City convenient to the rail transportation he needed to market his books and maintain his contact with the outside world. During this period of maturation as writer and publisher, he remained in close contact with his family in central Kansas and with extended family and friends in southern Illinois. He made occasional visits to Harlem and annual trips to Chicago where he visited friends and kept abreast of cultural trends. He probably subscribed to black newspapers including the *Chicago Defender*. The front page notice of his marital problems suggests that he was well known in Black

Chicago. Surely all of these contacts provided potential markets for his books.

Sioux City's railroad center also provided access to his former railroad colleagues. Pullman porters formed a small, close-knit community of individuals who remained in contact with each other for years. Newspapers like the *Chicago Defender* routinely carried columns devoted to news for railroad men.[162] Many of those men were well educated and served as leaders in their home communities, continuing to "run on the road" because better jobs were not available. Often they supplemented their income by other means, and among this group Micheaux might have found a ready source of agents interested in publicizing a book written by one of their own.

The Homesteader was Micheaux's third book. It was published in Sioux City in 1917, and on April 11, 1918, the Gregory *Times-Advocate* announced its availability to Rosebud residents:

> Oscar Micheaux, who was the only colored homesteader in this county, and has written considerable regarding his experiences on the Rosebud, has just completed another Rosebud story called "The Homesteader".[163]

The book is an unabashed reworking of *The Conquest*, but it delivers a different message and explores a fictional and melodramatic alternative ending. Gone are the details of homestead settlement, replaced by details of his budding writing career and by an account of Jean Baptiste's forbidden and suppressed love for "Agnes Stewart", this version's "Scottish girl", which he sublimates into the unhappy marriage with "Orlean McCarthy", the lascivious preacher's daughter.

While this retelling provided a measure of additional, accurate autobiographical detail, the ending turns on Orlean's tormented guilt over allowing her father to break up her marriage. The guilt results in her killing her father and committing suicide. By coincidence, Agnes meantime has learned that her dead mother had been an octoroon, thus making her an acceptable bride. Jean Baptiste marries her and they live happily ever after in the Rosebud.

The Homesteader was instantly popular with the public but had its share of critics. Perhaps because the material was deeply personal and thoroughly familiar, and because the writer was gaining skill, Micheaux spared the reader the convoluted, over-long agglomeration of plots and sub-plots that marred *The Forged Note*. The critics disliked the contrived and melodramatic ending that paid homage to the period's taboo against interracial marriages. Micheaux might have intended it as a social comment on the ridiculousness of acceptance or rejection based on "a single drop of black blood". Predictably, Chicago's black clergymen objected to criticism about one of their own.

Never one to dwell over-long on criticism, the implacable Oscar Micheaux continued his individualistic rise to success. With the success of *The Homesteader*, he found himself in the same position as a mid-20th century entertainer who "cried all the way to the bank". *The Homesteader* made money as a novel, and opened the way for an exciting and absorbing new career.

Over the next 30 years Micheaux would write, self-publish, and self-market four more books, often living for extended periods on their proceeds. In these works he described his life as a writer, self-publisher, and marketer, and made observations and social criticism about American society and the state of Black America. Taken together, the accounts provide insights and fruit for speculation about his life and personal philosophy. They also allow valuable glimpses into beliefs and circumstances common among African Americans in the first four decades of the 20th century and contribute details about the entrepreneurial system Micheaux devised and later adapted to keep his motion picture company afloat.

While they may not have contributed significantly to the world's legacy of great literature, they offer the Micheaux scholar a gold mine of information.

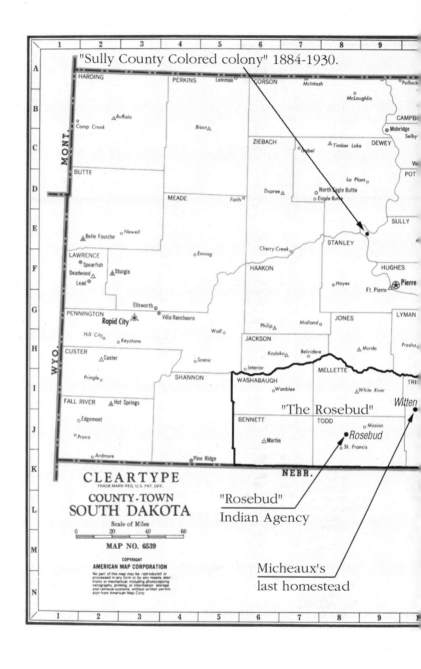

"Sully County Colored colony" 1884-1930.

CLEARTYPE
TRADE MARK REG. U.S. PAT. OFF.

COUNTY·TOWN
SOUTH DAKOTA

Scale of Miles

MAP NO. 6539

COPYRIGHT
AMERICAN MAP CORPORATION

No part of this map may be reproduced or
processed in any form or by any means, elec-
tronic or mechanical, including photocopying,
xerographic, printing, or information storage
and retrieval systems, without written permis-
sion from American Map Corp.

"The Rosebud"

"Rosebud"
Indian Agency

Micheaux's
last homestead

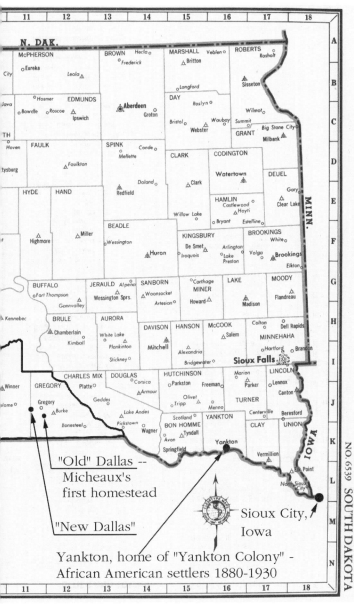

"Old" Dallas -- Micheaux's first homestead

"New Dallas"

Sioux City, Iowa

Yankton, home of "Yankton Colony" - African American settlers 1880-1930

"The Rosebud" counties are outlined and key locations identified. Sioux City, Iowa, (far right) was the site of Micheaux's first publishing company. While Micheaux, as an African American, chose to "go it alone", other African Americans settled in small farming or urban colonies in Sully county and at Yankton.

NO. 6539 SOUTH DAKOTA

Winner, South Dakota's Frontier Street Scene (1911). (Micheaux's "Victor" in *The Conquest*). Viewing the upstart, frontier Winner Main Street from the south end looking north to the newly developed railroad line. The Lambro State Bank building in the left foreground supports Micheaux's description of Winner's early business building development. According to Micheaux's narrative, after the railroad chose the Winner routing over the nearby town of Lambro, the business buildings of Lambro (Micheaux's "Amro") were immediately "jacked up" and conveyed with multiple-hitched horse and mule teams to the upper end of Winner's Main Street. (Dave Strain Collection, Rapid City, SD)

Gregory, South Dakota (Micheaux's "Megory"). Main Street looked like this in 1907, soon after Micheaux moved to the Rosebud. Note the offices of the Gregory *Advocate*, forerunner firm of the current Gregory *Times Advocate*, right.

Tripp County opened for settlement in 1909. Here, Mrs. Melcher, the lucky filer who drew #1 in the first day's drawing, sits proudly in the front seat of the automobile that will take her out into the county to select her home site.

Since 1996, Gregory County has honored Oscar Micheaux by re-creating his first homestead. A threshing machine sign on the south side of U.S. Highway 18, between Gregory and Burke, marks the road leading to the replica.

Members of the Gregory County Historical Society worked from Micheaux's description in *The Conquest* to help re-create his homestead. Twentieth century visitors to the little house get a taste of homestead life as they hear the ubiquitous prairie wind howling around the house and feel its draft through cracks in windows and walls.

The Exile, 1931. The first black-produced full-length "talkie".

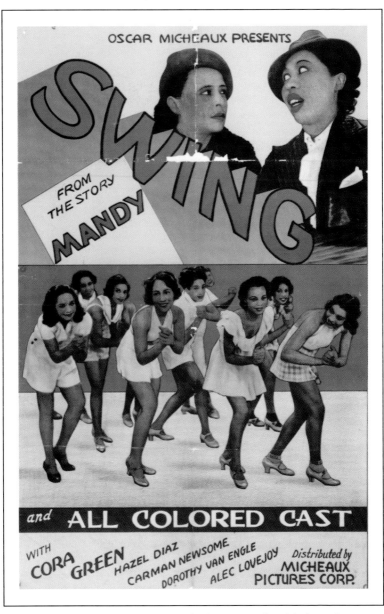

Swing, 1938. Cabaret scenes attracted white, as well as black, audiences to Micheaux's later films.

Courtesy of the Academy of Motion Picture Arts & Sciences, Margaret Herrick Library Collection.

PIONEER BLACK FILM MAKER & AUTHOR

OSCAR MICHEAUX

JAN. 2, 1884
MAR. 25, 1951

A MAN AHEAD OF HIS TIME

Oscar Micheaux's grave in Great Bend, Kansas, was marked in an official ceremony in 1988.

CHAPTER 7

THE FILM MAKER

Micheaux's *The Homesteader* could not have appeared at a more auspicious time. His persistent sales efforts had brought the book to the attention of African Americans across the country. Inevitably, film entrepreneurs would take notice.

By 1917, motion pictures had come a long way from their tenuous commercial beginnings in 1895. The Motion Picture Patents Company, a trust consisting of leading producers, finally had relinquished its strangle hold on the industry. That monopoly had successfully limited film lengths to one or two reels and refused screen credit to players. Now independent producers in Europe and the United States could form their own production and exhibition companies.

Fifty years of experimentation with visual toys like the stereopticon, the new projection device shown at the Cotton States Exposition in 1895, and the experiments in motion photography emanating from the Thomas A. Edison studios in New Jersey had prepared Americans for motion picture entertainment. Urban audiences, of immigrants and natives alike, were enthusiastic about the new movie houses where nickelodeons could run four shows every hour for a thousand viewers. By lucky accident, some of the experimental films shown in these houses portrayed African Americans in a wide range of roles, often showing them in a positive light. Included were scenes of the Buffalo Soldiers of the 9th Colored Cavalry, shot on location and portraying competent, dynamic black soldiers in American Army uniforms. Most presentations, however, were low comedy, often featuring ethnic or racial humor, or melodrama with stereotypical presentations of black people reminiscent of the old South or an Africa that never was.[164]

By the time the new white interests began to acquire technical and financial control over the industry and combined their
tiny studios into a national system, positive portrayals of blacks
had virtually disappeared. In the early teens, as the nation began
to recognize the fiftieth anniversary of the Civil War period,
Southern themes dominated in drama, in revisionist historiography, in Southern literature, and in popular culture, all aimed at
white reconciliation and a blurring of the past "unpleasantness".
The new emphasis placed the causes of the war on issues of economics and states' rights, and tried to ignore the divisive issues
of abolition and race relations, leaving former slaves and their
always-free brethren to continue their role as scapegoat.[165]

This did not deter African American interest in the new film
medium or their recognition of its potential. Already enterprising
theater owners in Chicago and other cities were offering new hits
to enthusiastic audiences in urban black communities. Beginning
about 1910, theatres in Chicago presented segregated screenings
for black audiences. Shown between midnight and 2:00 a.m.,
presentations included "race movies" or first run general audience films of interest to black viewers. The tradition of these
"midnight rambles" continued in some cities until desegregation
in the 1950s made them unnecessary. They offered opportunities
for audiences to view underground films dealing with controversial topics that represented "black reality".[166] Race organizations
like the newly-formed National Association for the Advancement
of Colored People (NAACP) and the Urban League saw the
national enthusiasm for cinema and recognized the danger posed
by filmmakers' stereotypical portrayals of the few blacks who
appeared in the films. As early as 1910, they began to express
concern.[167]

To be sure, dynamics in African American society contributed
indirectly to black distortion or omission. The race was proceeding on its uneven recovery from the effects of bondage, and
racial segregation patterns were hardening in both North and
South. The "Bookerism" controversy of accommodationism and
economic development versus political and civil rights, complicated by gaps between achievers and the poor, divided black
goals. These internal dynamics coincided with the refinement of

moviemaking techniques and reflected black responses to the
new industry.[168]

A few firms saw the potential for black-cast movies. In 1913,
Bill Foster, also known as Juli Jones, founded the Foster
Photoplay Company in Chicago, becoming the first African
American to establish a black-owned film production company.
He produced black-cast comedy shorts that opened to mostly
favorable reviews at Chicago's white-owned and black-managed
Grand Theater in July 1913, and in New York at the Lafayette
Theater during September. Foster's shorts appealed to the widest
segment of black audiences throughout the country. His black
perspective allowed African Americans to see themselves without
the superimposition of white stereotypes.[169]

Among the new white entrepreneurs, the most prominent
was D.W. Griffith, whose southern background and personal
racial biases combined with the tenor of the times when he
filmed the Rev. Thomas Dixon's controversial novel of
Reconstruction, *The Klansman*. The result was the ground-break-
ing *Birth of a Nation*, released in 1915. Griffith had made sweep-
ing advances in the technology. His functional use of the camera,
close-up techniques, and experimentation with lighting, camera
angles, lens filters, and timing of the action helped him create
exciting, rhythmic, well edited stories that captured public imagination.

The combination of Griffith's cinematography and the exciting, action-filled story gripped the nation for good or ill. *The
Birth of a Nation* was among the first to be lavishly promoted by
the new profession of press agents, and the scope and breadth
of the cinema production dazzled the critics. In New York, at the
Liberty Theatre on 42nd Street, background music was provided
by a 40 piece orchestra, and seats sold for as high as two dollars.
Attendance was a mark of high culture, and important Americans
were careful to be seen at its showings. Southern aristocrat
Woodrow Wilson, then President of the United States, a trained
historian and professional scholar, praised its accuracy. Press
agents exploited the presidential endorsement for three months,
despite his attempts to modify his support in the face of mount-
ing black outrage.[170]

The emerging civil rights and protest organizations, already concerned about retrograde racial attitudes in the Wilson presidency, rallied to a new and viable cause. For black Americans, there was no redeeming art in the presentation of a gothic horror story of Reconstruction that portrayed African Americans in type-cast stereotypes. With good reason, they worried that the film's appearance would create terrible, permanent, repercussions for black people at a time when lynching and repression were at their peak in both North and South.[171]

The resulting commotion included protests and picketing in New York and bitter clashes with politicians, policemen, and censors in Boston, as well as other protests across the country. Scattered victories resulted. The most significant occurred in Chicago where the support of the mayor, "Big Bill" Thompson, placed a black clergyman on the censor board. In several cities, protestors succeeded in tying censorship to anti-riot ordinances, a ploy that would backfire on Micheaux and others later. For the first time, African Americans presented a nationwide united front that boosted morale and generated great pride in the race. Although few white Americans understood what the fuss was all about, white film makers recognized that black audiences and black civil rights organizations were becoming forces to be reckoned with.[172]

None of this excitement escaped Micheaux's notice as he traveled the country marketing his books. No matter how isolated his location or what else he was doing, Oscar never lost touch with news of "the race". Hearing of the wild crowd outside his beloved Faneuil Hall in Boston when the eminent black publisher, Monroe Trotter, and other liberal politicians castigated Boston's leaders for their ineffective censorship of the controversial film aroused his blood and set his entrepreneurial mind a-working. Cripps suggests that the idea of producing motion pictures had already occurred to Oscar and he had, in fact, been experimenting with the medium.[173] Thus, while he might have been surprised when representatives of the Lincoln Motion Picture Company contacted him in 1917 about filming *The Homesteader*, he recognized the potential of the offer at once.

Lincoln was one of several companies that sprang into life in the wake of the protest movement. Some were only interested in providing an immediate antidote to *Birth of a Nation*; others saw themselves as the long term black answer to the growing white monopolies. The latter wanted to represent the "New Negro", urban African Americans who were coalescing into ghettos and building prosperous communities in white cities throughout the north. None of the firms could have prospered without that urban audience and its developing parallel black economy, newspapers, and community organizations. All would soon realize the formidable obstacles that would serve as barriers to their success. Lincoln, the second black-owned film production company, was among the most promising.

A group of Californians had launched the firm in Los Angeles in 1916. Noble Johnson, a contract bit-player at Universal Studios, was its chief executive officer. He doubled as director-scenarist and leading actor from 1916 to 1918. Other founding members included Dr. James Thomas Smith, vice-president and treasurer; Willes O. Tyler, attorney; and Dudley A. Brooks, assistant secretary. Clarence Brooks, the company's leading actor, served as secretary. In 1918, George Perry Johnson, Noble's brother and an Omaha postal worker, served as the company's general booking manager. The only white person affiliated with the company was Harry Gant, a Universal Studios cameraman.

The company wanted to produce long films for family viewing. The managers agreed with Foster that "blacks should make movies with black performers for black audiences... that there was a market waiting for such films and that the black entrepreneur would profit financially". Unlike Foster's company, Lincoln Studios concentrated on serious narratives with plots constructed "around a black rural hero's realization of some admirable ambition".[174] Oscar Micheaux's new novel, *The Homesteader*, seemed a perfect vehicle.

After seeing an advertisement in the *Chicago Defender* for *The Homesteader*, George Johnson wrote Micheaux's Western Book and Supply Company to inquire about film rights. In the exchange of correspondence that followed, Noble objected to certain themes in the work (perhaps the suggestion of inter-racial romance), but company officials assured the author that they could make a first-class feature film from the book.

Always sensitive to criticism of his work, Micheaux parried. In correspondence that survives in Lincoln's business records, he probed for information about the inner workings of the film industry. Already he had decided that his 500 page novel would not be confined to the Lincoln Company's usual two or three reel products. No less than a six reel "big picture" could do it justice. Inter-racial romance and marriage were controversial topics. A movie like *The Homesteader* that dealt frankly with the issue was bound to make money.

Eventually Micheaux broke off negotiations with the Johnsons and decided to make the picture himself. The Johnsons never forgot his slight, and forever disapproved of his business methods, style, and continual spats with censor boards, remaining nervous enough about him to maintain a spy in his office.[175]

Micheaux incorporated his operation under the name of Micheaux Book and Film Company and returned to the Midwest to give his old friends in Chicago and on the Rosebud an opportunity to purchase stock in his new film venture. He raised enough to make the film, bragging to the Johnsons that he had raised $5,000 in two weeks.

In Chicago, he rented the old Selig studio where he shot and cut it from scratch, adding a few location shots from the Rosebud taken at a farm near Winner. By the time he finished filming, he had begun to understand the craft, learning to prefer indoor shots because "the most subtle things go on in doors [sic]", and he began to seek actors that fit his types. He wrote about one actor, "Good face—bright [light skinned] complexion with good hair and my kind of Chin [sic]".[176]

Cripps remarked that Micheaux's

> brassy methods shaped *The Homesteader* into an event that other black producers envied. He landed the fine veteran of the Lafayette Players, Evelyn Preer, to give support to the rookies and amateurs who would make his epic of 'the Great American Northwest' and 'the race question'.

Amazingly, he was able to complete and release his new film in New York in less than two years, exceeding the efforts of managers at the faltering Lincoln company who, awaiting the opening of new facilities, shot film only on the weekends.[177] *The Homesteader* was the longest African American film to date and Micheaux knew he had a winner. Adapting the sales and promotion techniques that had enabled him to live off the revenue from his books, he devised a campaign guaranteed to draw black audiences to theaters all over the United States. He sold stock in the firm and scattered rumors that he had sold a book to Metro and Triangle, both prominent movie companies. Micheaux pushed his title with white theater owners who had black clienteles and with distributors.[178] The *Chicago Defender's* entertainment pages during this period provide a first-hand glimpse into the producer's evolving promotion techniques. From his new Chicago offices, known as the Micheaux Book and Film Company, Inc., at 8 South Dearborn, he kept news releases and paid advertisements flowing to the *Defender* and other race papers, timing the film's release to coincide with black Chicago's jubilant welcome of its own 8th Regiment (Colored) of the 370th Infantry, returning from service in France during the Great War. The *Defender's* February 22, 1919, edition devoted a special insert to their triumphant return, complete with pictures, interviews, and a history of their service to their country.

In a public relations coup, Micheaux announced that he would hold the premier of *The Homesteader* in the 8th Regiment's armory for four exciting nights. Theater goers could enjoy this experience for 50 cents on the main floor, 25 cents in the balcony. The *Defender* featured a half-page advertisement in the theater section of the paper, complete with photographs of the stars: lovely Evelyn Preer as Orlean, Charles D. Lucas as Jean Baptiste, Inez Smith as the evil sister, and fair-skinned Iris Hall as Agnes, the Scottish girl. Also pictured were George R. Garner, Jr., billed as "the race's greatest tenor, who will sing at each performance, with original music settings by David B. Peyton"; and Oscar Micheaux, author of *The Homesteader*. Conspicuous by its absence from the advertisement was the face of the actor playing Micheaux's nemesis, the Chicago clergyman.

Above the layout was a two-column, unattributed article entitled "'*The Homesteader*' Oscar Micheaux's Famous Story Makes Great Picture". It reviewed the story line and credited the film maker with a historic breakthrough, a "creditable, dignified achievement". A scathing two-paragraph indictment of the Rev. N. Justine McCarthy as "the embodiment of vanity, deceit and hypocrisy" was also included.[179] Evidently, this charge struck some members of the Chicago clergy as being perilously close to libel.

The next issue of the *Defender* carried a new unattributed article. It announced that *The Homesteader* was now playing at the Vendome, praised it as a "remarkable picture, both as to story and photography", and denounced the group of Chicago ministers who had sought to have it banned:

> Mr. Micheaux had a world of trouble in landing permits for his picture, it being necessary to go before the board with a committee of local people of standing, and to the credit of all concerned, be it said that they voted unanimously for the passing of it, favorable action being taken by the board of censors. This committee was composed principally of the following: Bishop Fallows, R.S. Abbott and wife [the editor of the *Defender*], Col. John R. Marshall, Oscar DePriest, Mrs. Ida B. Wells Barnett, Mrs. Lena Holt and N. Fields and Tony Langston [theater critic] of the *Chicago Defender*.[180]

The producer's half-page advertisement was similar to the earlier layout except that it proclaimed in large type: "Passed by the Censor Board Despite the Protests of Three Chicago Ministers WHO CLAIMED THAT IT WAS BASED ON THE SUPPOSED HYPOCRITICAL ACTIONS OF A PROMINENT COLORED PREACHER OF THIS CITY!"[181] (Considering that the correct name of the minister in question was N.J. McCracken, a name remarkably close to *Homesteader* minister N.J. McCarthy, the Chicago ministers might have had a point.)

Chicago audiences flocked to see the film when it played in
theaters around town all spring. The *Defender*'s entertainment
section continued to feature small advertisements that tracked it
to theaters in Macon and Atlanta, Georgia, Reidsville, North
Carolina, and a larger advertisement that announced it was
booked into Kansas City and St. Joseph, Missouri, Wichita and
Topeka, Kansas, and Omaha, Nebraska.[182] That same year
Micheaux presented the film to his enthusiastic former Rosebud
neighbors at the local theater in Gregory.[183]

George Johnson and Lincoln Film Company moguls were
amazed and outraged at their rival's quick rise from amateur to
studio chief. Micheaux had grossed more than $5,000 and now
had enough capital for his next project. His stock prospectus
named him president, novelist, and scenarist of the "Micheaux
Book and Film Company" with offices in New York, Chicago, and
Sioux City.[184]

Oscar had finally found his niche and already he was hard at
work on his next project.

Chapter 8

Building a Business

Micheaux's choice of subject for his second film reflected his desire to capitalize on the successful protests and provoke dialogue about American life. Although many consider *Within Our Gates* his answer to the *Birth of a Nation*, Oscar intended the film to respond also to the widespread general unrest in the aftermath of World War I.[185] It was a work guaranteed to create consternation among the newly sensitized film censors.

The war had mobilized civilians as well as military, and the new defense industries had placed diverse people from all races and backgrounds together in the work place and expected them to get along. Demobilization had destabilized that precarious balance, causing people of color to lose their jobs, and creating union movements that exploded into violence in the Pacific Northwest, resulted in police strikes in Boston and Washington, DC, and widespread general strikes in the coal industry. People worried also that the nationalist "anarchy" that gripped many European countries and destroyed the Russian monarchy would spread to the United States. This was especially frightening to "old" Americans, already suspicious of masses of immigrants from southern and eastern Europe.

In his study of public and private violence, Arthur L. Waskow writes that Americans remained reluctant to proscribe private violence. He describes how they had expressed that reluctance by placing assertions of "the right of revolution" in several state constitutions, and widely supported the political logic of the Second Amendment, which specified "the right of the people to keep and bear arms". It was a short step from that logic to a history filled with religious riots, vigilante hangings, labor dynamitings, private businessmen's armies, and southern lynching parties, all as half-accepted aspects of American life.[186]

The series of riots and civil disturbances that marred the entire year of 1919 questioned the roles of federal, state, and local governments in maintaining order. Uncertainties about handling these "incidents" led to experimentation with private armies, military peace keepers, paid strike breakers, and suspension of civil liberties. Fear and tension in many northern cities replicated the fear and tension black people in the South had faced daily since the end of Reconstruction.[187]

Although the labor-related incidents frightened officials and forced them to address new issues of law and order, more actual violence occurred that year as a result of the escalating conflicts between African Americans and whites. At least 25 incidents of racial violence occurred between the first incident in Berkeley, Georgia, in February and the last clash in Bogalusa, Louisiana, in late November. Most were expanded lynchings or brief clashes between sullen crowds, quickly dispersed. Seven, however, were major racial conflagrations.

The seven riots prompted an NAACP official to dub 1919 the year of the "Red Summer", an apparent reference both to its bloodshed and to the widespread fear that Russian Bolshevism had spread to the United States. Clearly, however, there was something different about this racial violence. Heretofore, the illegal but all-too-frequent lynchings and terrorizings of black people had been tolerated and seldom punished. Now, in 1919, the "New Negroes" were fighting back, and not just with protest movements.

The "Red Summer" began on May 10 in Charleston, South Carolina, and ended on September 30 with the Phillips County, Arkansas, riot. In between were explosions in Longview, Texas, Washington, DC, Chicago, Illinois, Knoxville, Tennessee, and Omaha, Nebraska. The Washington, DC, riot began on July 19, when a white woman, the wife of a service man, was allegedly assaulted by two African American men. Aggravated by a combination of irresponsible journalism by the *Washington Post* and other DC newspapers, a newly segregated federal civil service under the southern-oriented Wilson administration, and a large, restless, mostly white military population, the conflagration raged from Saturday until Tuesday night, resulting in several deaths, serious injuries, and widespread property damage. When cooler heads finally prevailed, Congress expressed the hope that it would not happen again but offered no solutions to the problems festering just below the surface.[188]

Shocked Americans, unused to seeing racial violence on the steps of their government, had no time to recover their equilibrium before the worst riot of that terrible summer erupted on Micheaux's very doorstep. On Sunday, July 27, not two weeks after the Washington debacle, a black swimmer at a Chicago bathing beach crossed the informal boundary between "white" and "colored" swimming areas and drowned under a hail of stones. When a white policeman ignored black requests to arrest the whites for stoning the swimmer, but instead arrested an African American on a minor offense, angry blacks mobbed the policeman. Word of the policeman's behavior spread and indignant black crowds, some with guns, began to fight back. The 13-day riot ended with 15 whites and 23 African Americans dead, 537 people injured, and enormous property damage and homelessness.

The violence forced the city to confront the long-festering conflict between white and black Chicagoans. The war had changed permanently the reasonably peaceful accommodation that had existed between the races. War-driven industry had attracted new workers, white and black, and more than 50,000 mostly rural African Americans from the South had swarmed into the city's Black Belt seeking work. The newcomers, many unprepared for city life, were willing to work for lower wages or to accept occasional employment as strike breakers, creating ill will and leading some unions to oppose their membership. Moreover, this huge migration stressed an already overcrowded housing situation, encouraging better-established African Americans to move into traditionally white neighborhoods. The shifting residential patterns had already created conflict over "possession" of public areas such as parks in some neighborhoods.[189]

The end of the riots brought a grand jury investigation that indicted 50 black and 17 white men, even though casualty figures suggest that more whites than blacks had used violence. In anticipation of bias against African Americans by the police, state's attorney, grand jury, and trial courts, black organizations mobilized to defend African Americans accused of riot crimes. Local and national representatives of the NAACP, the black Cook County Bar Association, the black YMCA, and the Urban League stepped in to ensure fairness. A Joint Emergency Committee of ministers and social workers concentrated on relief efforts and on attempting to collect damages for black citizens who had suffered property loss.[190] In addition to arranging legal defenses, all of these groups began a broad-based program to urge calm and improve the image of the Chicago black community. Posters and leaflets that appeared in black neighborhoods are instructive:

Listen to Me Fellows!
You all know Eugene F. Manns and you know
he is the only man in the Black Belt who Really
Does Big Things for You and Your Family. Now, fellows, let's all of us go home and don't stand around
the corners. As I am now in consultation behind
closed doors with the mayor and chief of police
fighting for you and your family's rights and arranging that all guilty persons who molested you be punished.
Yours for Good Luck
Eugene F. Manns
5003 S. State Street—
Te.[sic] Kenwood 8742

FOR NEEDY RIOT VICTIMS
FREE MEALS
at Olivet Bapt. Church
31st and South Park Avenue, Beginning
Saturday, August 2, '19
After 10 O'Clock A.M.
Dr. L.K. Williams, Pastor

Northwestern Book Co., Printers, 12 W. 27th St.

FELLOW WORKERS

We go back to work Monday 7:00 a.m. Sharp.
Use the Elevated Road, Keep Cool and Use your
heads. Remember loud talk never gets much else but
trouble. The riot is over. LET'S FORGET IT. We need
food and work for our families, so do you.
STEADY AND COOL IS THE WATCHWORD.
Signed
ARMOUR EFFICIENCY CLUB
MORRIS INDUSTRIAL CLUB
WILSON CO-OPERATIVE CLUB OF THE
WABASH
AVENUE Y.M.C.A.[191]

The fact that some Chicago leaders had been predicting violence for months suggests that Micheaux deliberately selected his
new script for its shock value. Moreover, its premier within
months of his first film implies that it either was shot simultaneously or immediately after release of *The Homesteader*. Thus, the
riot, with its aftermath of tension about lost jobs, property, and
housing, was occurring during the filming and release of *Within
Our Gates*. Micheaux's film came before the Chicago Board of
Movie Censors for approval in November, 1919, less than six
months after the riots had torn the city apart. When it was
released the following January, riot cases were still pending in
the courts.[192]

Still, the choice of story was a reasonable one. Like most
African Americans, Oscar was haunted by lynching as an insidi-
ous threat to black life and limb, one very difficult for blacks to
challenge. He was perceptive enough to understand the potential
of film as an agent of change. Earlier, his Atlanta book tour had
made him aware of the Leo Frank case of 1915, which he mentioned in *The Forged Note*.[193] In nearby Marietta, Frank, a Jewish
businessman, had been lynched by a mob for the alleged murder
of a young white girl employed in his pencil factory. Griffith's

violent *Birth of a Nation* and the current spate of national racial
violence gave new immediacy to Micheaux's topic.

The first advertisements for *Within Our Gates* appeared in the
Chicago Defender early in January, 1920, and featured Oscar's
standard publicity and promotion techniques. An unattributed
review in the theater section on January 10 described it as

> the picture that required two solid months to get
> by the Censor Board, and it is the claim of the author
> and producer that, while it is a bit radical, it is with-
> al the biggest protest against Race prejudice, lynch-
> ing and 'concubinage' that was ever written and
> there are more thrills and gripping, holding
> moments than was [sic] ever seen in any individual
> production... people interested in the welfare of the
> Race cannot afford to miss seeing this great produc-
> tion, and remember, it TELLS IT ALL.[194]

Within Our Gates depicts the lynching of a proud and successful black sharecropper, Jasper Landry, accused of murdering
his landlord, a white plantation owner. The lynching scene was
so graphic that censors initially rejected the film in fear it would
trigger more violence. A second viewing before a racially mixed
audience of prominent people produced a mixed response. Some
continued to object on the grounds that the film was incendiary.
Others who approved argued that it was time to bring the painful
truths to the attention of the general public. Alderman Louis B.
Anderson and Corporation Counsel Edward H. Wright were
prominent supporters of the film and their views finally prevailed.[195]

The dissenters did not give up gracefully. They launched a
campaign with the churches that included protestors who had
not seen the movie. Protests continued up to opening day when
a bi-racial delegation from the Methodist Episcopal Ministers'
Alliance visited the mayor and chief of police of Chicago to
protest, but retired without success. The picture opened as
planned at Hammon's Vendome Theater in Chicago, although initial turnout was disappointing. Cripps quoted Micheaux's corre-

spondence to George P. Johnson that reflected the producer's disappointment:

> "Our people do not care—nor the other race, for that matter," he complained, but he still expected to do movies that "leave an impression."[196]

Advertisements in the *Defender* continued throughout the month beside reviews and comments from local critics. Small advertisements tucked into the bottom of the entertainment section tracked its progress throughout the country from St. Louis to Atlanta, giving dates and theaters where it would be shown. In some cities, especially those with censor regulations tied to anti-riot ordinances, the film continued to create controversy.

In the south, theaters rejected the film outright because of its 'nasty story'. The white manager of the Star Theatre in Shreveport, Louisiana, refused to book the picture on the advice of the Superintendent of Police in New Orleans who asserted that

> ...the present Manager of the Temple [Theatre] stated [inaccurately] that he had witnessed this picture demonstrating the treatment during slavery times with which the negroes were treated by their masters, also show [sic] the execution by hanging of about nine negroes for absolutely no cause and that it is a very dangerous picture to show in the south.[197]

On January 31, the *Chicago Defender* published a bold-faced advertisement in the entertainment section just above the large paid photo advertisement for the film:

RACE PEOPLE OF CHICAGO - PLEASE NOTE!

> The Photoplay, WITHIN OUR GATES, was passed by the Censor, but owing to a wave of agitation on the part of certain Race people (who had not even seen it) 1,200 feet was eliminated during its

first engagement. This 1,200 feet has [sic] been restored and the picture will positively be shown from now on as originally produced and released with no cut-outs. — OSCAR MICHEAUX[198]

Although 1920 was a banner year for Micheaux and the company, primary and secondary sources do not reveal exactly what was happening in his life. Probably he was busy absorbing the daunting realities of his new business, including the terrible odds of booking pictures against the powerful white chains. Southern theaters in black neighborhoods would book black films in the slack summer season when the oppressive weather forced the major booking companies to shut down much of their operation. From May through July, Micheaux could depend only on one night stands, coupled with occasional split weeks, one full-week run in New Orleans, and a possible rebooking in Atlanta. Keeping his films booked required activity verging on perpetual motion.[199]

In spite of this pressure, Oscar managed to release three new films that year: *Within Our Gates, The Brute,* and *The Symbol of the Unconquered.* News of these releases appeared in the pages of the *Chicago Defender,* as did stories about his busy professional life. Together they raise interesting questions about production schedules for such an ambitious output.

On January 31, 1920, the same date as announcements appeared for *Within Our Gates,* the *Chicago Defender* reported Micheaux's next project.

GOING ABROAD
Noted Motion Picture Producer Soon
Sails for Europe

Oscar Micheaux, author and producer of "The Homesteader" and "Within Our Gates" will be in Europe 30 days from now. He is going abroad to arrange world distribution of his "Within Our Gates" and a series of new Racial [sic] features which he will produce upon his return. The first of these will

be "The Brand of Cain", which he has just completed in book form, and which will be published simultaneously with the release of the picture. Mr.
Micheaux states that plans are all complete for the
financing of these productions, which will be the
greatest achievement ever made by the Race. "The
appreciation my people have shown my maiden
efforts convinces me that they want Racial photoplays, depicting Racial life, and to that task I have
consecrated my mind and efforts."[200]

Meantime, work continued on his third picture, also a social
commentary. *The Brute*, a story about a prize fighter, dealt with
racketeering and with domestic abuse among African Americans.
An advertisement in the *Chicago Defender* on July 10, 1920,
offered a chance for Chicagoans to appear as "extras" during the
filming of the prize fight scenes at a staged match in the
"Beautiful Royal Gardens, 459 E. 31st Street, Chicago".[201]

On April 10, the newspaper featured a sketch about Oscar's
brother, Swan Emerson Micheaux, complete with photograph.
This article offered a glimpse of the inner workings of the
Micheaux Book and Film Company's shoestring business organization that was apparently struggling to consolidate its resources.
By now, a number of other black-owned companies had folded,
casualties of the catastrophic Spanish influenza epidemic that
coincided with the end of World War I, west coast isolation from
eastern audiences, or loss of financial support from white back-
ers. Micheaux, on the other hand, was on the verge of stability
and the announcement of his expanded organization may have
been intended to provide the necessary press and public relations support to ensure the firm's future.[202]

FINE CAREER

The subject of this sketch is Swan Emerson
Micheaux, favorite son of Great Bend, Kan., and
director and manager of the Micheaux Book & Film
Co. From the wilds of Kansas to the Loop, from

errand boy to film corporation manager is no small
jump. Mr. Micheaux has been and is a success at
both, despite the fact that he took over the management of the film company on the eve of its going
into the hands of a receiver. At the end of six months
he called the directors of the company to Sioux City,
Iowa, and cut the first melon, declaring 27 per cent
on a $40,000 investment. The report of this created
a sensation in Chicago's famous Loop. Experience
had stood him in good stead, and he took a chance
and made good. He knew that a concern of the [sic]
sort required real financial backing. He demanded
that the Board of Directors elect William Randolph
Cowan treasurer and that they raise the capital stock
to $100,000. He directed his brother, Oscar
Micheaux, to produce "Within Our Gates". "The
Homesteader" was the company's initial production,
and both are pictures that break all attendance
records wherever they are shown. It looks easy to
produce pictures, but to produce them and then
exploit them as an independent proposition requires
real selling ability. Young Micheaux recognized that
fact, set about securing men of the required ability,
with the result that today he has ten of the best Race
salesmen in the United States.

"There are three essential departments in the
picture game—unlimited capital, good productions
and selling management. The game is too fast for
slow thinkers. There must be quick action regardless
of cost, all hours working hours every day," said Mr.
Micheaux in a recent interview.[203]

Brother Oscar returned to Chicago on May 29, 1920, and the
Defender welcomed him home in another photo story.

PRODUCER RETURNS
Busy Making New Productions
Which Will Appear Soon

Oscar Micheaux, the prominent motion picture producer, who recently returned to the city after extensive traveling, during which time he has written a series of features as well as comedies, has already started the production of a new picture.

During his absence, Mr. Micheaux contracted with some of the most prominent and widely known actors and actresses of the Race; their names and photos will appear from time to time in these columns. He reports great activity in the building of new picture theaters by and for the Race in the East and South and the subsequent demand for more and better photoplays by Racial casts from stories concerning the lives of our people. The first new production will be ready about July 1.[204]

A careful reading of these news stories sheds no light on his previously announced film, *The Brand of Cain*, nor is it specifically stated that Micheaux was actually in Europe. Always a man of mystery, he understood the value of ambiguity. The three articles offer an interesting opportunity for speculation because it appears from the outset that the firm was teetering on the edge of bankruptcy. Micheaux kept afloat financially by personally peddling his films to theater owners and booking agents across the country. Although a trip to Europe was certainly possible, and his films became popular there and in South America, it is as likely that he spent those months touring the United States, making connections with theater owners and ensuring that his subsequent films would be played.

The Brute opened in New York in the late summer of 1920, with nine prints, every one "in action" in theaters both North and South. Obviously, the brothers' teamwork was paying off, promoting the opening while continuing to work on the next film. The company had prepared a polished publicity package consisting of lobby cards and stills, and the pre-release campaign guaranteed enthusiastic audiences. Most of the early critical notices were positive, although the crowds enjoyed the prize fights more than the message.[205]

A scant four months later, on September 28, 1920, the *Chicago Defender* published an unattributed review of *The Brute*, then premiering at the Vendome Theater to capacity crowds. This article cited it as the "biggest and best of the racial productions... in a class by itself... holds your interest from the first introductory title to the final fade out". Tersely summarizing the story line, the article pointed out the film's "extraordinary moral lesson" about the shame of spousal abuse and the perils of racketeering.[206]

Micheaux's next film, *The Symbol of the Unconquered*, followed quickly. Language in the *Chicago Defender's* January 8, 1921, article suggests that it first was released on the east coast before making its Chicago appearance at the Vendome on January 10.[207] Apparently the producer now was working at least part-time from the Morningside Heights address in Harlem that would serve as his headquarters and town home for many years.

This film is one of the few survivors. Until its recent rediscovery, contemporary scholars were not aware that an African American had written and directed a film that dealt critically with the Ku Klux Klan only a few years after D.W. Griffith's *Birth of a Nation*. Like the earlier *Within Our Gates*, the film contained a controversial sequence in which a black man and his wife were lynched, thus ensuring Micheaux's ongoing war with the censors.

The Symbol of the Unconquered continued Micheaux's lifelong exploration of "the West" as "the mythic space of moral drama and the site of opportunities seemingly free of the restrictive and discriminatory laws and social arrangements of the rural South and urban metropolis, where the characteristic model of economic expansion is entrepreneurship".[208] It is the tale of a beautiful quadroon woman's search for her western South Dakota inheritance, during which she encounters Hugh Van Allen, a gentlemanly black frontiersman who embodies the traits of the classic western hero. At first mistaking the heroine for white, and thus unavailable for marriage, he nonetheless assists her to recover her property which is found to contain valuable oil deposits. In a new complication, the villain, Driscoll, a quadroon passing for white, has "looked into her eyes", recognizes her as black and determines to drive her off her land. Van Allen, with true western chivalry, protects the heroine, saves her land, and ultimately learns that she, too, is legally black and is thus an appropriate mate.[209]

Again, Micheaux had tackled a controversial subject: the explosive consequences of miscegenation that "blurs the dichotomy on which whiteness depends...[and] throws into disarray the basis for white supremacy".[210] And, continuing his life-long pattern, Micheaux inserted his own role model persona. Hugh Van Allen is another reincarnation of Oscar Devereaux, Sidney Wyeth, and Jean Baptiste: strong and competent black men who, by their lives, reiterated the producer's life-long contention that "a colored man can be anything".

The film received high praise in the press. The *Competitor Magazine* opined that it "made a significant thrust at the more than 500,000 people in America who are 'passing for white'".[211] To be sure, "passing" was not a new phenomenon. In 1909, the *Daily Ohio State Journal* alleged that there were thousands of people "passing" in Washington D.C. alone:

> Those who just occasionally pass for white simply to secure just recognition, and the privileges the laws vouchsafe an American citizen should not be censured harshly. An unjust discrimination, a forced and ungodly segregation drives them to practice deception...But it is an awful experience to pass for white. At all times fear—the fear of detection— haunts one...Those who turn their backs upon their own color, own race and own relatives to live a life of fear, of dread, and almost isolation just to pass for white seven days in the week, while regarded with utter contempt by their colored race, really ought to be pitied, when it is known how heavy is the burden they carry, and how much they suffer in silence.[212]

Nonetheless, the film sparked heated debate by individuals and among community groups and, like previous releases, triggered the interest of censors, local sheriffs, and theater owners. By now Micheaux was accustomed to censor boards, and had developed techniques to circumvent them, routines that he would rely on throughout his long career. Frequently he capitalized on their censorial interest to increase attendance. For example, when *Within Our Gates* played in Omaha, his news release announced it as "the Race film production that created a sensation in Chicago" and "required two solid months to get by the censor board".[213]

In 1921 the company consolidated its offices in locations throughout the country. The production offices stayed in Harlem, where they had access to the largest collection of performers. The distribution and financial office remained in Chicago under the supervision of Swan Micheaux and Charles Benson, a former employee of the Quality Amusement Company. In Roanoke, Virginia, Tiffany Tolliver and W.R. Crowell operated a branch office in charge of east-coast distribution, while the distribution of films in the west was the responsibility of A. Odams, who owned the Verdun Theater in Beaumont, Texas.[214]

During those halcyon days of newly prospering northern black communities and close-knit southern enclaves of African Americans, when becoming "real Americans", fully accepted into American society, still seemed possible, black people were justly proud of their representation in films by and about themselves. The public and critics alike agreed that Oscar Micheaux's pictures were the epitome of fine race entertainment. Indeed, a 1920 review of *Within Our Gates* stood proudly as a reflection of those views and Micheaux's triumphant vindication for his belief in black achievement: "With proper directing such as we find in this super-picture, there is hardly a limit in screen work that we cannot reach".[215]

CHAPTER 9

THE STUDIO CHIEF

Lincoln Motion Picture Company folded in 1921, a victim of Universal Studio's pressure on Noble Johnson's contract and the lack of bookings in the west. That left Micheaux facing only one other serious rival, Robert Levy, the Jewish owner of Reol Pictures, whose power came from his role as "angel" to the famed African American Lafayette Players, many of whom transferred their stage skills to the screen. The few struggling firms that remained presented little competition for the two major survivors. Together Micheaux and Reol represented nearly half of the total output of the "race studios" that brought black cinema regularly to the eastern ghettos.[216]

Oscar could get $500 for each engagement in key urban houses: at the Lincoln in Cincinnati, the Vaudette in Detroit, the Comet in St. Louis, the Daisy in Memphis, the Regent in Baltimore, the Royal in Philadelphia, and the Dunbar in Washington. In New York, at the Lafayette, he once earned a gross of $10,000 on which he cleared $2000. He also booked his films into black YMCAs and schools, and could list more than 50 cities in which he could net $100-$500 per title. Always one to look after his money, he would accept $25 for a one-night stand in some tiny southern town, where his films were consistently popular. His earnings were $40,000 in 1920 and he hoped to earn $100,000 the following year.

The presence of Reol haunted Micheaux for the remainder of his career, as his 1920 remarks in a letter to George P. Johnson indicate:

Levy [Reol] and many other Jews who are making [N]egro pictures, going under [N]egro producers,
which they can afford to do because... they let the
pictures go for whatever they can get out of them,
too, there are so many bad colored pictures on the
market who are letting the exhibitors set the price
on their pictures [because]... the exhibitor finds that
the colored people will come to see a rotten [N]egro
picture as quick as they will to see the best
one.[sic][217]

Micheaux's resentment of these companies with their large
Jewish components would continue, to the extent that some of
his public remarks and some of the language in his later novels
reflect a bitter anti-Semitism that he always denied.

The new black studio chief was learning that white firms
could invade the black audience market profitably and at will. He
was also learning that African Americans presented a problematic audience. At this stage in the race's climb out of bondage, it
seemed that African Americans "simply did not *see themselves* on
the screen — even the screen of Oscar Micheaux".[218] Some black
critics recognized this phenomenon and puzzled about it. Other
critics simply were never satisfied. One Chicago reviewer panned
The Brute in a frame by frame analysis, remarking about a love
scene, "I didn't mind that, but the story was not elevating.... No,
Mr. Micheaux, society wants a real story of high moral aim that
can apeal [sic] to the upbuilding of your race".[219]

Other black critics, still enamoured of the stage, neglected
black cinema even when it was well done or, more hurtfully,
wrote positive reviews of black-cast, white-produced films and
ignored those produced by blacks. Radio, professional sports,
and recorded "race music" that became widely available in the
1920s further diverted public attention from cinema. Interestingly,
Micheaux's primary problem remained one of winning over a
skeptical black audience while struggling with a constant short-
age of capital. His few weapons were his boundless energy and
optimism and his success as a salesman. Nevertheless, to achieve
his goals, he needed to release three or four films a year.[220]

Oscar began the production of his next film, *Deceit*, at the Esste Studios in New York on June 6, 1921, basing the plot on his own unpleasant experience obtaining the Chicago Censor Board's approval for *Within Our Gates*. He followed that with *The Gunsaulis Mystery*, sometimes mis-identified by researchers as *The Gonzales Mystery* or *The Gunislaus Mystery*. This film continued his fascination with the Leo Frank lynching case and featured the film appearance of his alter ego, the semi-fictional Sidney Wyeth, protagonist in his novel, *The Forged Note*. In Wyeth's new incarnation, he was a black lawyer.

Also in 1921, the producer continued his long negotiation with Charles Chestnutt for the film rights to Chestnutt's popular novel, *The House Behind the Cedars*. The surviving correspondence between Micheaux's firm and the noted black author offers an interesting insight into the producer's business practices and was examined in detail by film scholar Charlene Regester. In 1920, George Anderson, Micheaux's assistant manager, had begun negotiations with Chestnutt, who was semi-retired and in poor health, but who expressed a cautious interest in the film venture.

When word of the negotiations leaked out, the Baltimore *Afro-American* applauded them, stating that "The collaboration of talents of a colored author and producer is unique and a step forward in establishing Negro standards in the films".[221] Although there is no evidence that Micheaux and Chestnutt ever met, their correspondence continued through Micheaux's intermediaries for nearly three years, and the 30 surviving letters provide insight about the difficulty of compensating authors and making movies in the under-capitalized world of black film making.

Chestnutt at first was flattered that his book might make a film, and his compliment to Micheaux on the quality of his films reflected the producer's current wide acceptance among the African American leaders. Undoubtedly the author was not prepared for the company's chronic financial difficulties. The original offer was $500 for film rights, which Chestnutt's publisher, Houghton Mifflin, thought was absurdly low. During the same period, white-owned Metro Pictures had offered $190,000 to

Vincent Blasco Ibanez for *The Four Horsemen of the Apocalypse*. Before Houghton Mifflin would approve the deal, they insisted that advertising materials always must state that the film was based on Chesnutt's novel "published by Houghton Mifflin". Micheaux's representative initially agreed upon the price but negotiated for a restructured payment schedule that, over the three year period, continually was revised, with payments frequently delayed. Negotiations dragged on and finally involved a concession that a serialized version of the novel would appear in the *Chicago Defender* prior to the movie. This occurred in 1921 and mollified both Houghton Mifflin and Chestnutt. It also whetted audience appetites for the film, which was finally completed in 1922, partially shot on location in Roanoke, Virginia.[222] Opening to good reviews, it broke all attendance records at the Roosevelt Theatre in New York City in 1923.[223] Two of Micheaux's most frequently featured actors, Shingze Howard and Lawrence Chenault, starred. The record shows that, as late as January, 1923, Chesnutt still had not received his final payment of $100.[224]

Once the deal was concluded, Micheaux freely offered the noted author advice about how to write better stories that would be more adaptable to the screen, suggesting that Chesnutt "write of the things you have known more intimately, I like stories of the South—strange murder cases, mystery with dynamic climaxes—but avoid race conflict as much as possible."[225] Regester suggests that one should not pass judgment too quickly on Micheaux's critical intent. While he did consider himself a true expert as a film scenarist, he might also have been concerned about film censor boards, or possibly about making films that could attract both white and black audiences and maximize the box office, or even what subjects would be most profitable in his already established audience markets in the south.[226]

During the negotiations with Chestnutt, Micheaux's film company was not idle, regularly releasing new films, many of which continued to address controversial themes. In 1922, however, the producer faced the first blast of criticism from a different quarter when he released *The Dungeon*, a seven-reel feature. This new attack came from the print media and might have foreshadowed a changing concept of racial "political correctness". The *Chicago Defender* chastised him for using light-skinned actors and not advertising the film as a "Race" production. On July 8, 1922, reviewer D. Ireland Thomas, black owner of the Lincoln Theater in Charleston, South Carolina, wrote:

> The advertising matter for this production has nothing to indicate that the feature is colored, as the characters are very bright; in fact, almost white. 'The All-Star Colored Cast' that is so noticeable with nearly every race production is omitted on the cards and lithographs. Possibly Mr. Micheaux is relying on his name alone to tell the public that it is a race production or maybe he is after booking white theaters.[227]

(Ironically, from the outset, Hollywood preferred its African Americans to be of darker complexion, although this was not widely discussed at the time. In a *Philadelphia Tribune* article on September 16, 1944, columnist Don DeLeighbur observed that until Lena Horne burst on the scene during World War II, Hollywood had a history of pronounced preference for darker skinned African Americans "because white people who pay the bills want to see only those Negroes of whom they are sure". He suggested that "the mulatto has been successfully discriminated against in amusement fields right down the line. Only three have escaped and broken into the really big time... Cab Calloway and the dance team of Maceo Thomas and Carol Chilton". He cited as examples of *dark* success Roland Hayes, Marian Anderson, Paul Robeson, Dorothy Maynor, Bill Robinson, and Ethel Waters. Those of lighter hue who were generally excluded were Fredi Washington, Jack Carter, Andrew Bishop, and Edna Thomas, the latter forced to play in dark make-up when she appeared opposite Helen Hayes in *Harriet* on Broadway.)[228]

Mr. Thomas liked Micheaux's 1924 film, *Son of Satan*, praising the acting quality in his review in the *Chicago Defender*. He commented that it had a more nearly "all star" cast than any other Race picture, but he warned that some viewers might object to some of the language as well as its portrayal of "some of our race in their true colors". Thomas concluded,

> I would not indorse [sic] this particular part of the film myself, but I must admit that it is true. We have got to hand it to Oscar Micheaux when it comes to giving us the real stuff... I am a hard critic when it comes to Race pictures, and... I do not want to see my Race in saloons or at crap tables.[229]

Not everyone agreed. Censors in Norfolk, Virginia, banned the film.[230]

Micheaux films continued to enjoy success, even though many African Americans, especially in the North, grew increasingly uncomfortable at film portrayals of their race, regardless of who produced them. During those anguished years when African Americans faced a continual barrage of white racism, there was considerable self-consciousness about how the race would be portrayed and perceived. Still, though his work often drew ruthless criticism and was forced to compete against white-made films emanating from Hollywood and shown in palatial studio-owned theaters, black people in the Northeast and South continued to constitute loyal, if often critical, audiences. Knowing that black entrepreneurs needed to develop stable businesses and industries, African American newspaper editors vigorously encouraged their readers to support these films and remained enthusiastic about the growth of the industry.

Film distribution remained the most serious logistical problem for all of the independents who were forced to compete with the large, well-funded, white-owned studios that controlled the nationwide distribution networks and owned many of the theaters. As the production companies gradually moved from the east coast to Hollywood, they built grandiose movie palaces all across the country to show off their work. In the balmy climate of Southern California, independent white producers like Thomas Harper Ince, Cecil B. DeMille, and Mack Sennett set up their own studios. They were well-financed and able to profit from economy of scale as well as the new management techniques that included the unit system, enabling a company to produce several films simultaneously through unit managers reporting to a studio head.

Production companies released hundreds of films each year to fill increasing demand from theaters. Like many of the "race movies", including some of Micheaux's, most were forgettable westerns, mysteries, slapstick comedies, or shorts, with an occasional elegant romantic melodrama or adventure story. They played in theaters in black neighborhoods as well as white. By 1921 there were more than 300 theaters in the United States catering mainly to black audiences. About half of these presented both vaudeville shows and films.[231]

Personal sales techniques were the black firms' best hope to compete with the film giants, even though the work of distribution was a tremendous drain on energy and capital. Micheaux's early experience with self-publishing and self-marketing his novels gave him a competitive edge in building an effective distribution system and taught him the value of an "image". From the outset, he presented himself as the Studio Chief, a man of means and importance. A hefty six-footer of enormous dignity, he wore tailored black suits and enjoyed distinctive long Russian-style, fur trimmed coats and extravagant wide-brimmed hats. He traveled in a chauffeur-driven limousine. Although he might not have had more than a few dollars in his pocket, he appeared to be a wealthy man. He learned to make his arrival on scene an event, "stepping out of cars and into meeting halls as if he were God about to deliver a sermon".[232] One of his long-time actors, Lorenzo Tucker, once said, "Why, he was so impressive and so charming that he could talk the shirt right off your back".[233]

Donald Bogle credited this charm and sales skill for Micheaux's success in persuading Southern theater owners to show his films. He would begin a sales pitch by telling them of the new black audiences and their willingness to spend money to see black-cast films. When he spoke of possible profits for the theaters, managers listened. Micheaux films became staples at special matinee performances for black audiences, repeated at midnight for white audiences interested in an inside view of black life. Aware of white fascination with black night clubs, he began to include in his films cabaret scenes that would appeal to whites.[234]

Over the course of a few years, Micheaux had begun to assemble a company of actors, some of whom stayed with him for many years. Others remained long enough to be noticed by white studio managers and then left for Hollywood. At first he chose his casts from existing theater companies like the Lafayette Players in New York. Later he found them in unusual places. Legend indicates that sometimes he would spot a figure, or note a gesture, or the way light fell across a face, and sign the individual up then and there.[235]

He was not an easy man to work for, and collecting their pay was often problematic for cast and crew who needed to be paid on time. Over the years, black actors commented appreciatively about the opportunity to work, but expressed great frustration about whether they would be paid. On one occasion, his competitors at Lincoln Motion Picture Company received a telegram from a dissatisfied, unnamed Micheaux employee:

> MICHEAUX STATES MAKING YOU PROPOSITION DON'T ACCEPT BELIEVE ME I AM FOR YOU AND IN A POSITION TO KNOW HIS UNBUSINESSLIKE METHODS BEYOND COMPARISON HAVE HIM BOOKED UNTIL MIDDLE JULY BUT CANNOT STAND HIM ANY LONGER [236]

Other problems preoccupied the studio chief. As a businessman and technician, he kept abreast of the latest trends in the industry, although usually he had insufficient capital to invest in them. Changes in film technology, typical of any new industry, and the desperate need for time, financing, and training to absorb and use the new techniques created an impossible situation for black filmmakers who knew in the cutting room that there was "something lacking" in their techniques. Bad lighting concealed action, unmatched textures marred shots filmed under varied conditions, jerky rhythms interrupted the story line, poor staging destroyed the effects of a shot sequence. Cripps pointed out that all of these problems could have been corrected by shooting at a higher ratio of exposed film to usable film, by retakes, and by using a master cover-shot from which to cut to varied angles and closeups. None of the filmmakers could afford such luxuries, much less employ a competent film cutter who could edit a bad shot or control pacing and texture by careful selection, nor, most of the time, even afford the luxury of retakes. Micheaux tried hard and sometimes succeeded better than most, but competition from better funded and better-trained white film makers in Hollywood became a serious problem.[237]

To meet his self-appointed schedule of four releases a year, Micheaux often resorted to a variety of techniques and schemes. Like the Hollywood studio moguls he despised, for every carefully conceived, thoughtful picture he released, hoping to entice increasingly sophisticated and skeptical black audiences, there would be forgettable films intended to provide mindless entertainment and pay the bills. Sometimes he saved money by writing the stories and scripts himself.

When all else failed and he was short of cash, he reworked a previous film, sometimes patched together from out takes, or merely re-titled and re-released. This practice created serious problems for film scholars attempting to determine exactly how many films the Micheaux Film Company produced. When the news editors took note of his potboilers, they commented on the size and enthusiasm of the audiences rather than on the film's artistic merit (much as they did with comparable B or C pictures emanating from Hollywood).[238]

As the years went on, Micheaux struggled to find themes that would appeal to disparate black audiences and still put forth his disputed beliefs about the problems, cures, and future of the race. Scholars have marveled at his survival in the face of adversity. Other "race" companies died or moved out to Yonkers. He stayed in Harlem, where he kept his people working while developing and presenting new talent, and producing credible films despite brushes with bankruptcy.

By 1926, Micheaux had 17 films to his credit, including the silent film, *Body and Soul,* one of only a few that survive. It appeared in 1925 and starred the famed actor and singer Paul Robeson. Cripps considered this picture one of Micheaux's

strongest, because of its message as well as acting, arguing that
for the first time Micheaux "wrestled with the nature of the black
community, without recourse to shoddy devices, overdressing in
the good cloth of Dunbar or Chesnutt, or inter-racial sensationalism". This film was his graphic, controversial commentary on the
ghetto "jackleg" preachers "who exploited the deep religiosity of
poor blacks who settled in cold ghettos and turned to the charis-
matic churches as visible proof that their old Southern rural lives
still had meaning". The story exposed those "cultist parasites"
along with bootleggers and gamblers, and suggested that black
people could organize against unwholesome forces in their
midst.[239] One could also argue that this film was simply one more
attack on his perceived hypocrisy of the black church and the ex-
father-in-law who had cheated him.

Not only did *Body and Soul* provide opportunity for black
people to see one of their own highly talented and widely recognized personalities in a black vehicle, it also was the screen
debut (and apparently single appearance) of Julia Theresa
Russell, who soon would be Oscar Micheaux's sister-in-law.
Romance apparently had entered the producer's life in the person of Julia's sister, actress Alice Bertrand Russell. Very little information has been collected about Alice Russell, but there is sufficient evidence for speculation about her increasing importance in
his life.

She first appeared in the screen credits for Micheaux productions in 1926, when she played in *The Broken Violin*. She
appeared in other Micheaux pictures: *Wages of Sin* in 1928, *When
Men Betray* in 1929, *Daughter of the Congo* in 1930, *The Girl from
Chicago* in 1932, *Lem Hawkins' Confession*, a reworking of the
old *Gunsaulis Mystery* with sound and music in 1935, *God's
Stepchildren* in 1938, and Micheaux's final picture, *The Betrayal*,
in 1948.[240] Later, her name would appear as producer of several
Micheaux films, and apparently she edited his later books.

The date of their marriage has been variously reported.
Sampson writes that it occurred in 1929, and other biographical
sources agree. Lee Arlie Barry, however, cites the 1928-29 issue
of *Who's Who in Colored America*, which gives the marriage date
as March 20, 1926.[241] Several sources agree that the couple

bought a home in Montclair, New Jersey where they set up housekeeping, and from which they conducted a portion of Micheaux's later business. Russell became his business partner, at one point shielding the firm from bankruptcy by placing its assets in her name.

It might be significant that after her appearance on the scene, brother Swan left the Micheaux Film Company. On March 1, 1927, he became a manager of imported films of the Agfu Raiv Film Corporation of Berlin, Germany, with offices at 729 7th Avenue, New York City. After a year at that job, he became Vice President and General Manager of Dunbar Film Corporation, located at 440 Lenox Avenue, New York City.[242] Later, he made a film of his own, *Midnight Ace*, that achieved modest success.

Sampson recorded the Micheaux company's experience with bankruptcy in February, 1928, when the "Micheaux Film Corporation, with offices at 200 West 125th Street, filed a voluntary petition of bankruptcy in the U.S. Seventh District Court. The petition listed the assets of the company as $1,400 and liabilities as $7,837".[243] Perhaps this voluntary bankruptcy allowed the firm to refinance and reorganize its assets to invest in the new sound technology.

Hollywood producers had released the first sound pictures as early as 1926. Warner Brothers used a process known as Vitaphone, which recorded musical and spoken passages on large discs that then were synchronized with the action on the screen. They released *The Jazz Singer* in 1927 to enthusiastic audiences, but by 1931 the technology was already obsolete and soon replaced by the more flexible "Movietone" system that recorded sound directly on film in a strip beside the picture. Micheaux, always a forward-looking man, would have been eager to take advantage of this revolutionary system.

In any case, he reorganized the company in the latter part of 1929, creating a new firm under the laws of the State of New York, with Oscar Micheaux as President, Frank Schiffman as Vice President, and Leo Bracheer as Treasurer. This move brought white money and white control into the company.[244] Harley W. Robinson, Jr., believes that this white influence, as well as the wishes of white owners of theaters in black neighborhoods, might have affected Micheaux's future choices of stories and casting selections.[245] In keeping with the racial stereotyping of the period, light skinned actors often played roles of heroes, while darker complexioned actors often appeared as villains. Sometimes black critics objected strenuously to these casting choices as non-representative of African American culture.

Mark A. Reid argues that reorganization shifted Micheaux's productions from "black independent" to "black commercial", thus signalling an end to black independent film making that would not resume until the 1970s.[246] In 1930, the reorganized company produced *Daughter of the Congo* in which Micheaux's wife appeared. In 1931 the *New York Age* reported, "While Mr. Micheaux remains the titular head of the motion picture company, the control has passed into the hands of the lessees of the Lafayette and other theaters in Harlem."[247]

The next year his company released its first "all-talkie" film, *The Exile*, a major accomplishment for a struggling independent film company still perceived by Micheaux and his public as black-owned, despite the infusion of white money. In addition to a cast of "old dependables", the film featured a number of singers and dancers from the stage reviews, *Blackbirds* and *Brown Buddies*, and from night clubs like Connie's Inn, and the Cotton Club. There were enough cabaret scenes to interest both black and white audiences.[248]

The story takes place in Chicago at a time when an influx of southern black migrants was pushing out wealthy white property owners along South Parkway. The central plot deals with a proper young black man whose fiancee had inherited the ownership of a South Parkway mansion that had become a combination cabaret and brothel. Appalled, he flees to the plains of South Dakota where the story continues in a variation of the ubiquitous autobiography. There he meets a young woman whom he assumes to be white, befriends her, and loves her from afar until he learns that she has Negro blood and all ends well.

Sampson reported that *The Exile* had a successful premiere in New York City, although in Pittsburgh two female members of the Pennsylvania Board of Censors successfully stopped the show because it did not carry the seal indicating passage by the

State Censor Board. Viewers speculated that the real reason for
stopping the show was that it contained scenes showing a Negro
making love to a "near white" woman. Had the ladies from the
Censor Board paused to review the end of the picture, they
would have seen that the woman in question actually had one
per cent Negro blood. In another scene, viewers saw a white man
forcing himself on the woman and soundly thrashed by the black
hero who came to her rescue. Eventually the film cleared various
censor boards and enjoyed a long run, but the problem continued to point out Micheaux's lifelong fascination with the "near-
white" and the easily-documented controversy such evidence of
race mixing produced in both the black and the white world.[249]

The company released four films in 1932, including *Veiled
Aristocrats*, a sound version of *The House Behind the Cedars*. The
title was an example of a technique often found in Micheaux's
films and books: the borrowing of a character's name or title from
another artist's work. In this case, *Veiled Aristocrats* was the title
of an unrelated 1923 novel by Gertrude Sanborn.[250]

After 1932, the company's annual production slowed to one
or two pictures a year until 1940. With two or three notable
exceptions, they were forgettable, and reflected both the Great
Depression and the terrible financial and talent pressures that
independent film makers suffered as the Hollywood studio system raised standards to take advantage of changing times and
technology.

For several years beginning in the late twenties, Hollywood
film makers had briefly opened their doors to black entertainers
and drawn away the best-known black stars from the independents. Evelyn Preer, who started with Micheaux and appeared in
most of his productions, left for an opportunity in Hollywood,
expressing great admiration for Micheaux but maintaining that
"colored actors would get their best chances from white directors."[251] Preer had several good years in Hollywood, but they
ended with the Depression. Her experience was similar to other
black actors whose staying power in Hollywood did not survive
the economics of the thirties.[252]

Nevertheless, California was a powerful magnet. It was the
home of the "talkies" with access to the latest technology and

arguably the best directors. Big company owners, anxious to show off their sound technology and choreographic expertise, were excited about using Negro talent. Theirs was a textbook example of stereotyping in action: "everyone" knew that Negroes could sing and dance better than whites, that their dialect and colloquialisms and quaint sense of humor amused whites, and that black voices were uniquely compatible with talkies' technology. According to Reid, the author of one article observed that "as a casual example of what the motion picture industry [Hollywood] means to Los Angeles Negro citizens by way of employment and its effect upon their economic situation, one studio paid $2,307 to colored extras last week." The next year, the same publication finally admitted that black producers, music composers, and singers were "hard hit" by the Depression.[253]

Even while operating within these constraints, the Micheaux Film Company produced three films that deserve mention. In 1938, *God's Stepchildren* returned to the theme of color prejudice and passing. Micheaux utilized a common theme in black culture of the period, reflected in the African American press and a variety of short stories — the personal, sometimes tragic, identity crises faced by light skinned individuals attempting to find a "place" in a racially divided America. The story deals with a very light skinned girl who refuses to accept her race and "acts out" so that she is placed in a convent for 12 years. On her release, she marries a dark skinned Negro, gives birth to a boy, deserts him to her foster parents and slips into the white race. Here she marries a white man, who eventually learns her secret and rejects her. Returning home in disgrace, she commits suicide by jumping in the river.[254]

Micheaux had used this controversial "passing" theme before. It also formed the plot of popular late-twenties novels such as *Quicksand* and *Passing* by Nella Larsen and *Plum Bun* by Jessie Fausset, both respected black writers of the Harlem Renaissance.[255] Apparently, by 1938 ideas of "political correctness" were undergoing revision, because the film was greeted by a storm of protest at its world premier held at the RKO Regent Theater in New York City.

The film company withdrew it after only two days at the theater, and RKO later prohibited its showing in any RKO Theater in the country. Subsequent showings of the film in other theaters were preceded by an announcement of the ban and included a follow-up statement from Micheaux that all objectionable parts of the picture had been deleted. It appears that viewers objected in part to the level of violence. Many walked out during the scene when an actor, playing the part of a white man, knocked down a young girl and spat upon her because she had revealed that she had "colored blood". Among groups protesting the picture were members of the Young Communist League and the National Negro Congress, who objected that it "creates a false splitting of Negroes into light and dark groups... and slanders Negroes, holding them up to ridicule".[256]

In 1939, Micheaux released *Lying Lips*, a large cast cabaret melodrama that featured Robert Earl Jones, father of James Earl Jones, as a detective. To appeal to white audiences as well as black, the producer laced it with cabaret singing and dancing. It is one of only a handful of his films that survives.

The country was gradually creeping out of its paralyzing economic depression, but the upswing did not help the independent producers of race movies in their constant struggle for capital. Improved technology and increased audience expectations meant that productions cost more, and the independents rarely could raise a "nut" higher than $40,000. This was not enough money to compete successfully, especially in advertising, where they could afford only poorly laid out press books that did little to attract business. To complicate matters further, Hollywood was beginning to understand that African American audiences represented important sources of revenue and gradually they were opening doors to more black players. Toward the end, only Micheaux and one or two others hung on in the face of the white establishment's unyielding barriers. In the words of Thomas Cripps, Micheaux had survived "rural naivete, conniving exhibitors along the Mississippi Valley circuits, the burdens imposed by disused studios, personal bankruptcy, charges of misappropriation, bad scripts, artless movies, indifferent actors, and the life on the road".²⁵⁷ It was a losing battle, even for as skilled an entrepreneur as Oscar Micheaux.

On New Year's Day, 1940, Micheaux released what was to be his next-to-last film, one he hoped would be among his best. He had a new partner, Colonel Hubert Julian, a colorful character known as the "Black Eagle". Julian was an aviator who had achieved recognition while flying for the embryonic Ethiopian Air Force. He had also tried unsuccessfully to follow Lindbergh's trans-Atlantic flight, and was a vigorous campaigner in the struggle to require the Army to accept black aviators. Together they planned to be the "dream team", producing movies that would, in Julian's words, "build up the morals of my race". Already they had collaborated on *Lying Lips*.

The new film, *The Notorious Elinor Lee*, was intended to be a tribute to blacks who had helped to restore the popularity of boxing. Robert Earl Jones played the role of a great African American boxing champion who had obligated himself to the underworld. The crooks had assigned Elinor Lee, played by Edna Mae Harris, to soften him up to persuade him to lose the fight. The film opened in New York at the RKO Regent with a glamorous Harlem premiere attended by glittering black stars who had responded to gold engraved invitations. The "Black Eagle" appeared at the premiere as master of ceremonies wearing formal dress: top hat, white silk gloves, and a flowing cape. There were floodlights, a carpeted sidewalk, and police. Homage was paid to Mayor Fiorello LaGuardia's encouragement of movie making in New York. Unfortunately, the picture was a disappointment, failing to live up to its promise, and the box office returns were slim.²⁵⁸

Perhaps tired of his new partner, certainly tired of the business, frustrated by the competition and the constant struggle for money, Oscar Micheaux called it quits. He began an eight-year hiatus from film making and returned to his other love: writing, publishing and marketing his books.²⁵⁹

Ironically, just as Micheaux was giving up his long film making career, word of its successful history filtered back to South Dakota. On March 4, 1940, the Sioux Falls *Argus Leader* published a feature story about his success:

NEGRO WHO HOMESTEADED IN ROSEBUD
NOW BIG MAN IN U.S. MOVING PICTURES

Burke, S.D., March 4, 1940. A large number of
people from all over the Rosebud will be glad to
hear again of Oscar Micheaux, one of the few Negro
homesteaders on the Rosebud, who later wrote a
number of books, one of which was "The
Homesteader" which dealt with homestead life on
the Rosebud. Mr. Micheaux homesteaded southwest
of Burke. Gus Matousek, an early day homesteader
who was later connected with the business interests
of the Rosebud and now is with the Joint Stock Land
Bank with headquarters in Decorah, Ia., at a recent
fieldman's meeting in Chicago called on Ernest
Jackson, also widely known throughout the Rosebud
as being a member of the firm of Jackson Brothers
who made Dallas [SD] famous in the early days.

Mr. Jackson told about the present abode and
prosperity of Mr. Micheaux. He stated that he had
risen high in the movie producing industry, and that
two-thirds of the movie houses in the Negro district
of Chicago continuously show "Oscar Micheaux
Productions". He lives in New York and drives to
Chicago in a 16-cylinder car with a white chauffeur
[sic]....

In talking with Mr. Matousek, Jackson said: "I
associate him [Micheaux] in my memory with a big
horse and two small mules, the outfit he used when
the Rosebud was building. How times have
changed." [260]

CHAPTER 10

THE HIDDEN YEARS

In self-published editions of his books, Oscar Micheaux often included a preface or an acknowledgement that offered clues to his current circumstances or personal philosophy. On other occasions, dialogues by his fictional alter egos served a similar purpose within the context of his novels. Bowser and Spence observed that, even though his work left these clues, it is impossible to tell whether they represent the "real Micheaux" or whether they are simply another part of his carefully constructed biographical persona.[261] Nevertheless, they are worthy of examination and consideration.

There is, for example, his description in *The Case of Mrs. Wingate* of his frustration with the motion picture business. In the persona of Sidney Wyeth, black motion picture producer and novelist, he described that disenchantment in a manner that might well have expressed his state of mind.

> During the past year or so, the picture business had been slowly dying. Their pictures had all been "played out", and Wyeth... had been pushed out of making pictures by Jewish interests from the Pacific coast, and other Jewish interests in the east, who felt it could be made very profitable... [Wyeth's firm] had been dependent almost entirely for more than a year on the sale of the book that Wyeth had written, set up a company to publish, and was fortunate enough to get it going before they went entirely broke as picture producers....[262]

Four books written during this final period include his most accomplished, *The Wind from Nowhere*, a novel that updated the homesteading story, setting it sometime later than the 1920s. It was published in 1944. Two detective stories with story lines that complemented each other followed in 1945 and 1946. His final book, *The Masquerade*, was an unapologetic re-telling and modification of Charles Chestnutt's *The House Behind the Cedars* that appeared in 1947.

By the time these works appeared, people knew Micheaux primarily as a film maker. The books attracted little critical notice, although they sold well among his loyal followers. Journalist Richard Gehr wrote that *The Case of Mrs. Wingate* sold 50,000 copies and topped the black bestseller list when it appeared.[263]

All four books bore the marks of the film scenarist and script writer accustomed to thinking and writing in scenes, action, plot, and sub-plot. Literary critics were quick to point out that his writing skills and technical mastery of the craft had not improved significantly. These might have been weakened further by a new, unpolished, earthiness that seem to reflect a prim man's attempt to be "modern". Little wonder that scholar David Levering Lewis, writing of the Harlem Renaissance, dismisses Micheaux's work as "curious folk novels".[264] Reviewing literary critics describe versions of the stories that this writer, reading carefully, failed to recognize. Only the most persistent reader can trace plot and sub-plot through pages of extraneous dialogue that do little to advance the story line.

Nevertheless, this material provides evocative glimpses into hidden aspects of black life during particular eras. Just as the reader of *The Forged Note* can vicariously walk the streets of the Atlanta, Birmingham, Memphis, and New Orleans ghettos in the teens, the reader of his later books can view a wide variety of black lifestyles in Chicago, Memphis, and Harlem during the twenties, thirties and forties, and glimpse, if only briefly, the world of the black independent film producer.[265]

Readers also can glimpse Micheaux's persona through the actions, conversations, and soliloquies of Sidney Wyeth or Martin Eden, Micheaux's alter egos who appear in the later novels. Wyeth, the protagonist in *The Forged Note*, had appeared also in at least one Micheaux film (as a black lawyer in The *Gunsaulis Mystery*). In the companion detective stories, Wyeth returns as the former homesteader turned novelist, motion picture producer, and book seller. These stories, although obviously written for the pulp market, merit examination for their popular culture-based perspectives on the race question as well as on Micheaux's personal experiences.

In the first, *The Case of Mrs. Wingate*, a Georgia white girl (Mrs. Wingate) falls in love with a black barber whom she cannot marry. Instead, she weds an impotent but wealthy old man (Wingate) and, on his death, uses her inheritance to hire the barber as her New York chauffeur, whom she then sends to Harvard to acquire a Ph.D. As a frustrated professional with an impractical education (Micheaux's bias against professional training for which there were few job opportunities), the erstwhile barber becomes friends with Wyeth while flirting with fascism as a cure for American racism.

The politics of the over-educated barber-turned-activist bring him into contact with an attractive mixed-race brother and sister from Germany who are undercover agents for the Third Reich. They have come to the United States under orders to subvert American Negroes for the coming war, and to kill Eleanor Roosevelt when the opportunity presents itself at one of her frequent appearances in the black community. The former barber and the male spy approach film maker and novelist Sidney Wyeth, and request that he make a propaganda film in support of fascism. The ethical Wyeth refuses, despite his floundering motion picture business, which is in trouble because of the unscrupulous Jewish element controlling the Hollywood film industry.

When Wyeth meets the spy's charming sister, he falls in love with her at once. Becoming suspicious about the siblings' politics, and suspecting subversion, Wyeth manages to learn about the plot that is intended to force his now unwilling lady love to kill Mrs. Roosevelt. Wyeth arranges with a black detective friend to foil the assassination plot and arrest the male spy. This protects Wyeth's sweetheart, saves Mrs. Roosevelt, and leaves Wyeth free to marry his new love, an innocent dupe trapped in the spy ring because of her evil brother.

Because of his writing style and his inclusion of other characters and sub-plots in the story, critics seem to have missed Micheaux's primary story line, concentrating instead on the Georgia widow's infatuation with the black barber and the distracting insertion of a pair of black lovers whose marriage has been prevented because of the woman's insistence on an acting career. The critics' reaction seems to be a reflection of white society's incredulity about race-mixing, the misleading title, and their preoccupation with the quiet Harlem wedding of white Mrs. Wingate to her black protege.[266]

In *The Story of Dorothy Stanfield*, Wyeth's detective friend returns as the protagonist in love with the beautiful and mysterious Mrs. Stanfield, and is assigned to investigate an insurance fraud. Wyeth, the detective's confidante, is now married to the former spy and the couple entertain Mrs. Stanfield on her visit to New York, where she also meets the former Mrs. Wingate and her new black husband.

The story line of this detective novel, however, deals primarily with the insurance fraud for which Mrs. Stanfield's alcoholic physician husband has been jailed. Micheaux based his fraud case on an actual incident in St. Louis in 1926, when a barber was apprehended for his collusion with a crooked undertaker in series of fake interments that allowed the fraud ring to collect insurance benefits for old paid up policies on living people.[267] In Micheaux's story, the ring consists of the physician, Dr. Stanfield, who has debased his reputation by performing illegal abortions, a crooked undertaker, and a down-at-the-heels entertainer willing to be buried alive and subsequently dug up in exchange for a share of the payoff.

Both the German spy story and the insurance fraud story require an element of suspended belief but might not be as preposterous as they appear to the casual reader or the white literary critic. With respect to the German-Negro spies, Micheaux utilized obscure, but factual, circumstances following World War I that left a few soldiers from Africa in parts of Germany, where some married local girls and stayed. Under those very temporary conditions, it is marginally plausible that before Hitler's racist regime was widely recognized, a young, smart, bi-racial protege might have temporarily captured the attention of a rising government looking for ways to subvert and conquer American democratic institutions by taking advantage of American racism. Obviously, such an individual would not have survived Hitler's final solution, once he had served his purpose, and Micheaux's scenario allowed that probability.

Critics also objected to the likelihood of an intelligent, young southern "colored man" — a barber, no less — becoming the protege and eventual husband of a lovesick Georgia white woman of independent means. Yet anyone with any day-to-day experience of life in any northern urban ghetto, as early as the beginning of this century, certainly becomes aware of inter-racial couples, frequently with southern roots, who had quietly assimilated into the middle and upper class black world and made reasonable lives for themselves.

Critics also have been troubled by aspects of the third book, *The Wind from Nowhere*. Some have expressed boredom with Micheaux's persistent return to the South Dakota story of his early youth. Reasons for his lifelong fascination with the homesteading experience and that thwarted love affair continue to invite speculation, but will probably never be fully understood. This version of the story, like *The Homesteader*, is presented as a romantic novel, differing from *The Conquest*, which appeared as a bare-bones disguised autobiography. Critics commented disapprovingly about Micheaux's choice of Martin Eden as the name for his alter ego and protagonist because it was the name chosen by Jack London for the hero of his semi-fictional autobiography, *Martin Eden*.[268]

As in the case of his film, *Veiled Aristocrats*, Micheaux often appropriated fictional names or titles as well as actual circumstances. Examples include the fund raising activities that created black YMCAs in the late teens in *The Forged Note*, the insurance fraud portrayed in *The Story of Dorothy Stanfield*, and the identification of one of his lady friends in *The Wind From Nowhere* as "Jessie Binga," which happened to be a feminized version of the name of a prominent black Chicago banker, Jesse Binga, who regularly advertised his institution in the *Chicago Defender* in the early years of the twentieth century.[269] Appalled critics puzzled over his apparent need to rewrite Charles Chesnutt's successful *House Behind the Cedars* under the title of *The Masquerade*, his last book.[270] Because he had purchased the film rights from the now-deceased author, Micheaux apparently had no compunctions about rewriting the story with a happy ending.

More curious still is Micheaux's explicit, thinly disguised, pejorative commentary on contemporary African Americans. Two egregious examples appear in the detective stories. Wyeth, in his role of motion picture producer, novelist, and book seller, avows that his firm handles books by many popular authors. Some in his "stable" closely parallel actual individuals. The novel's characters then proceed to dissect these well-known, but thinly disguised, public figures in forceful and pejorative language that borders on the libelous.

For example, in *The Story of Dorothy Stanfield*, there is a long dialogue between Mrs. Stanfield, private detective LeBaron, and a mutual friend, teacher Bob Martin. The topic is inter-racial marriages and the harm those liaisons are doing to "The Race". Several pages of diatribe deal with the lifestyle of a prominent African American author named "Frank Knight", who had married a white Jewish woman and absented himself from black society after achieving fabulous success with sale of his books to whites and a few blacks. The books are entitled *Nature's Child* and *Black Narcissis* and are particularly distasteful to the speakers because they describe the seamier aspects of black life and dwell on race prejudice. The fictitious author thus castigated seems to be a loosely disguised reference to Richard Wright who had achieved both critical and financial success with his books, *Black Boy* and *Native Son*, and who at that time was allegedly flirting with Communism.

The speakers contrast "Frank Knight"'s behavior with that paragon of virtue, Sidney Wyeth, whose book, *The Homesteader*, is concerned with more uplifting themes. Wyeth is, in the words of one of the speakers, "about the only Negro engaged in writing fiction who is free and independent in what he writes …and who writes about us colored people as we are living and thinking today... who puts the love and romance of our lives into his stories".

Later, LeBaron and Martin discuss the career of a shady physician named "Dr. Thurston" who has a sister named "Ora" who "calls herself an anthropologist". Ora had begun by attending Howard University and studying journalism, and gone on "to develop into an adventuress". She had married several times and had "let herself develop temperament and was on the way to a controlled insanity... became too educated... wrote five books all published by a major publishing house... then went into the business of acquiring scholarships, awards, and into so many ways of getting money from white people... Sidney Wyeth told me that none of her books ever got out of the first edition, which means that they did not sell well. The last I heard of her she was said to be living with some rich white family in Hollywood but that didn't last, either, for she has been back in New York since...". This description bears a remarkable resemblance to aspects of the life and career of the critically acclaimed African American writer and folk anthropologist, Zora Neale Hurston.[271]

Most troubling to readers and critics of the day, however, was Micheaux's insistence on portraying black people in improbable roles and circumstances for their time and place. Most white critics "knew" absolutely that black people did not have successful careers as lawyers, detectives, insurance executives, large western land owners, self-published writers, motion picture producers, or race leaders who achieved their position because of educational and cultural assistance from wealthy, infatuated white women willing to risk all for love. White scholars familiar with the Harlem Renaissance, however, knew about wealthy white patrons of both sexes who provided money, encouragement, and other benefits to promising young black writers and occasionally attached "strings" that restricted their personal and artistic freedom and created internal psychological conflicts.[272]

To be sure, the world of financially successful African American professionals and businessmen in major metropolitan cities of both North and South was largely hidden from white view before the civil rights movement of the 1960s. Urban centers of black life like Chicago, Harlem, Los Angeles, or Raleigh-Durham, North Carolina, and old, predominantly black settlements like Tuskeegee, Alabama, or Boley, Oklahoma, boasted a solid core of successful black professionals in many walks of life. Indeed, a discerning and persistent researcher can find similar examples hidden in obscure state or county histories. Even in remote, homogeneous South Dakota, one can find the occasional wealthy black rancher, farmer, or businessman who enjoyed independent financial success and a measure of public respect until the vicissitudes of an unpredictable economy created permanent setbacks or caused him to seek greener pastures elsewhere.[273] Thus, readers and critics should not be too quick to claim that Micheaux's characterizations were impossible, although they might have been rare.

Studies in New Social History that examine historical periods from the "bottom up" instead of the "top down" are performing the important service of accustoming the American public to a new awareness of the existence of improbable but actual circumstances surrounding ordinary people. These workaday folk are not often the ones who keep diaries, write history, or capture headlines. Within such a paradigm, Micheaux's black spies, lawyers, detectives, and wealthy businessmen or farmers, while admittedly rare, are not impossible. Even if they were only marginally plausible, Micheaux might have argued that it was important for "The Race" in general and white folks in particular to suspend belief long enough to recognize that these improbable scenarios would become probable for tomorrow's black children.

Micheaux wrote in the preface to *The Case of Mrs. Wingate* that he frequently found himself defending his books from critics who objected to the frequency of the race-mixing theme. "Race-mixing is not the theme of Mr. Micheaux's novels by any means," he argued, "but its mere presence in the novels has led to the books' rejection by many reviewers, in spite of their popularity". He defended the middle-class setting of his novels by asserting that such images are never found in works by other writers, white or black. "Except in his novels," Micheaux wrote, speaking of himself in the third person, "the Negro is never shown as a contemporary American citizen, talking as most colored people have

long been speaking, in plain and simple English. In the matter of
romance, he seems presumed not to have any whatsoever".[274]
    We know very little about where and when Oscar Micheaux
wrote his later books. Perhaps he worked at the couple's home
in Montclair, New Jersey. We know that his wife helped edit them
and prepare them for publication and assisted with their sale and
distribution.
    While Oscar enjoyed his life as a writer, the world of film was
never far from his mind. As Hollywood came under increasing
pressure from Walter White, Executive Director of the NAACP, to
change its portrayal of African Americans, Micheaux joined black
film maker William D. Alexander and author Richard Wright in
volunteering his support of White's efforts. During the years of
World War II, as external pressure from African American organizations mounted and was joined by the federal Office of War
Information (OWI), Hollywood struggled to project a new racial
image. Among those who complained to OWI that "only a tiny
fraction of wartime film 'shows the Negro from any standpoint'"
was Oscar Micheaux. He offered his experience to the film makers as "one who had 'learned how and what to do to get [blacks]
into the war spirit'".[275]
    Toward the end of his eight-year hiatus, Micheaux was
tempted back to the film industry. Some felt that it was a mistake
to try to turn his moderately successful book, *The Wind from
Nowhere*, into a film. Many critics stated unequivocally that he
should not have attempted a comeback. It was, after all, a reworking of *The Homesteader*, produced this time by white-
owned Astor films, directed by Oscar Micheaux and titled *The
Betrayal*. This time his wife, Alice Russell, appeared in the cast.
The project began in 1948 when Micheaux was 64 years old,
tired, and suffering from severe arthritis that required the occasional use of a wheelchair. In *Making Movies Black*, Thomas
Cripps described his last efforts:

    ...sickness and poverty were already eroding his
    chutzpah. As his wife reported to her sister, "Dad
    has arthritis all over his body, but he keeps going."
    In pain, stiffened, swollen, he plodded on, seeming

to live on nervous energy and on the hope that a return to the Middle Western roots would restart his engines. "Dad saw that the Book business was going down," his wife wrote, "so he decided that he would try to get back in Pictures... Therefore he took all his little money and went to Chicago." There, almost home... [he imposed] upon himself the burdens that had spoiled every one of his most personal movies. The book was as big as a dictionary, and invincibly resistant to boiling down... and he chose [for his players] an uneven mix of schoolteachers, a radio actor, a dancer, and an understudy in *Anna Lucasta*, thus ensuring that the movie would wear a caste mark peculiar to the genre—an ensemble so varied in talents as to jangle against rather than complement each others' work.[276]

Such a difficult project demanded the most of a healthy man. He spread himself too thinly, commuting to New York with the "dailies", straining his health and strength and facing financial ruin in one grand gamble. "He is doing it all alone," his wife told her sister. "Isn't that wonderful?"[277] Unfortunately, it was not. When he drove the rushes to the airport for the flight to New York, others took over in his absence. A member of the crew recalled, "We were having money problems all the time, so on Sunday we'd go out and sell books" or try to pre-book the unfinished film in Peoria or Joliet.[278]

He spent the winter in New York, cutting the film, preparing the final version, writing advertising copy, and trying to raise the last $500 he needed for completion money. The result was a critical disaster. Although black audiences reportedly enjoyed the film, Cripps stated that "black critics almost wept and felt that the film never should have been shown". One of them "wished to sneak away and hide in a corner" rather than face its "acting worse than amateurish, the dialogue ridiculous, the story downright stupid". White critics agreed. One of them wrote, "monumental incompetence, a preposterous, inept bore... less artful... than home movies".[279]

Sick and in pain, Micheaux returned home to his wife. Critics were allowed to write the finis to a lifetime of hope, struggle, and entrepreneurial success.

Oscar Micheaux suffered a heart attack and died on a promotional trip to Charlotte, North Carolina, in 1951.[280] His wife retreated to their New Jersey home, sealed his records, and apparently lived out her life quietly on the east coast.

In the face of this secrecy, very little detail has come to light about Micheaux's later life except in occasional quiet reminiscences from family, some of whom, when contacted by scholars, expressed surprise at his rediscovery and claimed to have few details. Harley W. Robinson, Jr., now an octogenarian and a successful and widely traveled Los Angeles insurance broker and former military man, will, when pressed, speak warmly about his cousin, Oscar, whom he often visited at 25 Morningside Drive, New York. Micheaux was a good host and enjoyed showing the young man around the city, always ending their visits by admonishing young Robinson to "stay in school and make something of yourself".[281]

It was Harley who remained concerned that Oscar Micheaux's grave in the family burial plot at Great Bend, Kansas had been left unmarked. When a special fund-raising drive to correct that oversight was sparked by members of the newly emerging black film colony, Robinson handled the details, including extensive and appropriate newspaper coverage and coordination with state and local historians.

In a graveside ceremony on October 8, 1988, attended by fans and members of the Kansas State Historical Society, a gray granite headstone was placed on the grave. Appropriately, it is inscribed:

Oscar Micheaux

1884-1951

"A Man Ahead of His Time"

AFTERWORD

The Civil Rights movement that reached its apex during the turbulent 1960s began to bring African Americans into the mainstream of American life and culture. It was not long before the effects were felt in the national popular culture of movies and that rapidly growing medium of mass communication, television. Gradually, white Americans became accustomed to seeing people of color in different and interesting roles and, over time, talented black entertainers found increased opportunities to showcase their skills before mixed-race audiences.

As television took over American living rooms and left movie theaters dark, the Hollywood studio system began to collapse. New, young film makers found freedom to tackle unusual and controversial issues and film scholars began to mine the archives of the old studios, and to study, with new appreciation, the evolution of the American film genre. African American artists like Harry Belafonte, Sidney Poitier, Esther Rolle, James Earl Jones, Ossie Davis, Ruby Dee, and Gordon Parks were joined by newcomers Bill Cosby, Oprah Winfrey, and others. Together they began to represent a significant source of economic and financial reserves that continues to provide African Americans with freedom to explore the race's history in the entertainment business, and specifically, in the world of film.

By the early seventies, bold, young African American directors like Spike Lee, Eddie Murphy, Robert Townsend, and Melvin VanPeebles were stepping into the shoes long-vacated by Oscar Micheaux. Their films presented the black world from an insiders' perspective and contained much the same level of outspoken social comment that characterized the best of Micheaux's work. It was natural for these African American newcomers to seek their roots by studying the work of the early black independents, especially Micheaux. In 1974, the Black Filmmakers Hall of Fame was created to honor distinguished African Americans in the film industry, including posthumous recognition of the early pioneers. They established the prestigious annual Oscar Micheaux Award for excellence.

In the late seventies and early eighties, a spate of articles about black participation in the film industry began to appear in the popular press, bringing general readers the information that the scholars had been painstakingly collecting. Among the earliest was a lead story in the February, 1988, issue of *Ebony*, entitled "Black America's Rich Film History". Author Dalton Narine painstakingly pointed out that

> ...the contemporary contributions of Eddie
> Murphy, Spike Lee, and Robert Townsend are reflec-
> tions of a history that goes back to the silent film era
> and the breakthrough movie, *The Homesteader*, the
> first film directed by a black. The year was 1918 and
> the man was Oscar Micheaux, a film maker who
> wrote, produced, directed, and even distributed his
> own movies....[282]

Although some of the early articles reflected contemporary attitudes of "political correctness," deploring Micheaux's political and social ideas and identifying flaws in his technical competence, there was general agreement that he was important as a pioneer entrepreneur in the infant film industry. Gradually, as copies of his lost films were found, remastered, studied by the film scholars, and compared with other early independent films, respect for his vision and skill has grown among his peers, resulting in many posthumous honors. In 1987, the "Avenue of the Stars" in Hollywood dedicated a star on its sidewalk to "The Father of Independent Black Filmmaking", Oscar Micheaux.

Eventually, an account of this awakened interest reached Micheaux's old homesteading country in an article that appeared in the Sioux Falls *Argus Leader* on February 21, 1989:

When the Black Filmmakers Hall of Fame hon-
ors its best this afternoon in California, it will be
working with a South Dakota connection. The Oscar
Micheaux Awards Ceremony is named after a South
Dakota homesteader who became the nation's first
black filmmaker... The 15th annual Micheaux
Awards will be presented at 2 p.m. in Oakland, Calif.
The Hall of Fame was organized in 1974 to preserve
black contributions to film and black filmmakers...
Sammy Davis, Jr. was among those inducted into the
Black Filmmakers Hall of Fame...Oscar Micheaux
was posthumously honored with the Directors Guild
of America's Golden Jubilee Special Directorial
Award. He is the first black American director to be
so honored. "At last a black man and film director
has been given the recognition he so richly deserves
by his peers in the film industry," said Wendell
Franklin, a guild member who made the presentation. The Hall of Fame, established in 1974, also
received a rare 15-minute segment from Micheaux's
1932 film, *Veiled Aristocrats*....[283]

Study of Micheaux's work continues throughout the film
industry and academia. An over-arching organization, The Oscar
Micheaux Society, is an international group based at Duke
University that keeps Micheaux devotees current through the
publication of a newsletter begun in the early nineties.

In March, 1995, the *Chronicle of Higher Education* featured
Micheaux in an article that established him as the leading pioneer
black filmmaker and credited him with breaking the racial stereotyping common to Hollywood studio casting. That article drew
parallels between Spike Lee and Micheaux, suggesting that Lee's
shuffling of chronological events in *Pulp Fiction*, characterized by
critics as "bold", was nothing more than what Micheaux had been
doing in the 1920s.[284]

Micheaux's work has been recognized in other ways, including the outstanding documentary that made its debut on public
television in the fall of 1995. *Midnight Ramble* was a critical suc-

cess and an outstanding labor of love by black film scholars, presenting the detailed story of the development of black-cast films,
and focusing its entire second segment on the work of
Micheaux.[285]
    On September 24, 1995, the *New York Sunday Times* pub-
lished an article captioned, "The Marquee is the Message".

>   On film, a movie marquee sometimes peeks out
>   of the background then quickly disappears.... During
>   the first moments of *Devil in a Blue Dress*, a period
>   thriller opening on Friday that stars Denzel
>   Washington, the director Carl Franklin pays homage
>   to one of his idols with a marquee that announces
>   "The Betrayal". The film was made by Oscar
>   Micheaux, the pre-eminent black film maker of the
>   1920s and 30s... But the literal reason was that at the
>   time there was a substantial black film-going com-
>   munity, and Micheaux catered to that.[286]

    Recently, African American author Columbus Salley, Ed.D.,
Superintendent Emeritus of the Newark, New Jersey, Public
Schools, wrote a book entitled *The Black 100*, an enumeration
and ranking of "...The Most Influential African Americans, Past
and Present". Dr. Salley's intent was not to begin a debate on the
"most talented" or "most influential", but rather to identify the
men and women of giant talents who had the most widespread
and critical impact on black progress toward full participation in
American society.
    His collection included the obvious: Dr. Martin Luther King,
Jr., Harriet Tubman, Frederick Douglass, Booker T. Washington,
W.E.B. DuBois, Paul Robeson, Malcolm X, Thurgood Marshall,
Joe Louis, Muhammed Ali, Bill Cosby, and many others, each
assigned a ranking based on Dr. Smalley's perception of the value
of their contributions. Number 81 in this interesting and highly
readable book is Oscar Micheaux, chosen for his success as an
entrepreneur in circumstances that would have destroyed a less-
er man, his role as the dean of the black filmmakers, and his out-

standing influence in presenting a broad view of the diverse lifestyles of black Americans.

Dr. Salley's ranking suggests that in spite of general and widespread criticism of Micheaux's preference for the black middle class, his images balanced and countered the negative images of Hollywood. He further suggests that much of the criticism Micheaux encountered resembles the late twentieth century criticism of Bill Cosby, who pioneered the use of television to offer a broader image of African American lifestyles and values.[287]

Not surprisingly, Oscar Micheaux offered the best summary of his own life's work and his approach to film making in a signed article that appeared in the *Philadelphia Afro-American* on January 24, 1925.

> Unless one has some connection with the actual production of photoplays, it is impossible fully to recognize the tremendous scope which the motion picture embraces. The completed picture is a miniature replica of life, and all the varied forces which help to make life so complex, the intricate studies and problems of human nature, all enter into the physical makeup of the most lowly photoplay.

> The mastery, therefore, of the art of production, for indeed it is an art, is no small attainment, and success can only be assured when assisted by the most active encouragement and financial backing. The colored producer has dared to step into a world which has hitherto remained closed to him. His entrance into this unexplored field, is for him, trebly difficult. He is united in his themes, in obtaining casts that present genuine ability, and in his financial resources. He requires encouragement and assistance. He is the new-born babe who must be fondled until he can stand on his own feet, and if the race has any pride in presenting its own achievements in this field, it behooves it to interest itself, and morally encourage such efforts.

I do not wish anyone to construe this as a request for the suppression of criticism. Honest, intelligent criticism is an aid to the progress of any effort. The producer who has confidence in his ideals, solicits constructive criticism. But he also asks fairness, and fairness in criticism demands a familiarity with the aims of the producer, and a knowledge of the circumstances under which his efforts were materialized.

I have been informed that my last production, BIRTHRIGHT, has occasioned much adverse criticism during its exhibition in Philadelphia. Newspapermen have denounced me as a colored Judas, merely because they were either unaware of my aims, or were not in sympathy with them. What then, are my aims, to which such critics have taken exception?

I have always tried to make my photoplays present the truth, to lay before the race a cross section of its own life, to view the colored heart from close range. My results might have been narrow at times, due perhaps to certain limited situations, which I endeavored to portray, but in these limited situations, the truth was the predominant characteristic. It is only by presenting those portions of the race portrayed in my pictures, in the light and background of their true state, that we can raise our people to greater heights. I am too much imbued with the spirit of Booker T. Washington to engraft false values upon ourselves, to make ourselves what we are not. Nothing could be a greater blow to our own progress.

The recognition of our true situation, will react in itself as a stimulus for self-advancement.

It is these ideals that I have injected into my pictures, and which are now being criticized. Possibly
my aims have been misunderstood, but criticism
arising from such misunderstanding, only doubles
the already overburdening labors of the colored producer.

If I have been retarded by the unjust criticism
from my own race, it has been amply made up by
the aid of the Royal Theatre [sic], which from the
very beginning, has encouraged the production of
colored photoplays, and in the face of burning criticism, has continued to foster my aims, and help
place my organization on a strong footing.

It is only by constructive criticism, arising from
an intelligent understanding of the real problem,
however, that the colored producer can succeed in
his efforts and produce photoplays, that will not
only be a credit to the race, but be on a par with
those of the white producer.

...[signed] Oscar Micheaux.[288]

Thus, we have come full circle: from the initial excited appreciation of Oscar Micheaux's pioneering efforts in the new medium, to disparagement based on the technological superiority of
white competition and the maturing self-image of African
Americans that became reflected in the way white Americans
considered black people, to rediscovery of his work by film
scholars, and now to a renewed appreciation of the man and his
work by Americans of all races.

Thanks to the tireless efforts and dedication of the film scholars, the African American artists and entrepreneurs, and the great-
grandchildren of the Rosebud homesteaders, a new generation of
writers, film makers, earnest young entrepreneurs, and the
descendants of those who settled the Rosebud will glimpse again
Micheaux's undying vision — appropriately modified in language to encompass our growing egalitarianism — "that a colored man can be anything".

APPENDIX

OSCAR MICHEAUX'S FILMS

1919 *The Homesteader*

1920 *Within Our Gates   The Brute   The Symbol of the Unconquered*

1921 *The Gunsaulis Mystery   Deceit*

1922 *The Dungeon   The Virgin of the Seminole*

1923 *Jasper Landry's Will* (sometimes known as *Uncle Jasper's Will*)

1924 *Birthright   Son of Satan   The House Behind the Cedars*

1925 *Body and Soul*

1926 *The Spider's Web   The Broken Violin   The Conjure Woman   The Devil's Disciple*

1927 *The Millionaire* (featuring a cameo appearance by *Chicago Defender* publisher, Robert Abbott)

1928 *Wages of Sin   Marcus Garland   Thirty Years Later*

1929 *When Men Betray*

1930 *Easy Street   Daughter of the Congo*

1931 *The Exile* (first black-produced "talkie")   *Darktown Revue*

1932 *Veiled Aristocrats* (remake with sound of *The House Behind The Cedars*)   *Black Magic*   *Ten Minutes to Live*   *The Girl from Chicago*   *Ten Minutes to Kill*

1934 *Harlem After Midnight*   *The Ghost of Tolston's Manor*

1935 *Lem Hawkins' Confession* (*The Gunsaulis Mystery* with sound)

1936 *Temptation*

1937 *Underworld*

1938 *God's Stepchildren*   *Swing*

1939 *Birthright* (a remake with sound)   *Lying Lips*

1940 *The Notorious Elinor Lee*

1948 *The Betrayal* (Astor Films, with Micheaux directing)

(Source: Sampson, and Micheaux internet home page: www.geechee.com/Micheaux.html)

OSCAR MICHEAUX'S BOOKS

Micheaux's seven books include:

The Conquest: The Story of a Negro Pioneer by the Pioneer (Lincoln, Nebraska: Woodruff, 1913; reprint University of Nebraska Press, Lincoln, Nebraska, 1994.)

The Forged Note: A Romance of the Darker Races (Lincoln, Nebraska: Western Book Supply, 1915.)

The Homesteader (Sioux City, Iowa: Western Book Supply, 1917; reprint University of Nebraska Press: Lincoln, Nebraska, 1994.)

The Wind from Nowhere (New York: New York Book Supply, 1944.)

The Case of Mrs. Wingate (New York: New York Book Supply, 1945.)

The Story of Dorothy Stanfield, Based on a Great Insurance Swindle, and a Woman (New York: New York Book Supply, 1946.)

The Masquerade: An Historical Novel (New York: New York Book Supply, 1947.)

Note: Readers interested in Mr. Micheaux's out of print books can be accommodated through an inter-library loan search. A number of university libraries retain circulating copies; others hold non-circulating copies which may be read on the premises.

Readers can also obtain information about the Oscar Micheaux Society and its newsletter by contacting the Duke University Program in Film and Video, 107A Art Museum, Duke University, Durham, North Carolina 27708. (919-684-4130, FAX 919-684-3598).

The Oscar Micheaux Society of Gregory, SD, presents an annual Oscar Micheaux Festival in Gregory each August. The five-day festival celebrates Oscar Michaeux's life and work, as well as the homesteading and town-building experience on the Rosebud. Many humanities scholars and entertainers interested in film history, African American history and culture, and the Great Plains homesteading experience attend and participate in a variety of activities each year. The public is invited to attend and share the experience. Interested readers may contact Richard Papousek (605-835-8002) or Francie Johnson (605-835-8391, e-mail: johnson@gwtc.net).

END NOTES

¹For a complete listing of Micheaux's novels, see the Appendix.

²Frazier, E. Franklin, *Black Bourgeoisie: The Rise of a New Middle Class*. (New York: MacMillan Publishers, 1957), p. 19.

³Oscar Micheaux. *The Wind From Nowhere*. (New York: New York Book and Supply, 1944), pp. 17-18. Note: This phrase is repeated throughout Micheaux's writings and was a foundation of his personal beliefs.

⁴With the exception of *The Conquest*, which is now coming into its own as an accurate memoir of railroading, South Dakota homesteading, and the politics of town building, generally critics have not been kind to Micheaux's books. (Refer to "Oscar Micheaux: The Melting Pot of the Plains", by Arlene Elder; *The Old Northwest: A Journal of Regional Life and Letters*, Volume 2, No. 3, September 1976.) David Levering Lewis, who chronicled the Harlem Renaissance, dismissed the homesteading novels as "curious folk novels", perhaps because the subject matter was so far outside the ken of the Harlem milieu. Like other critics, he ignored the four later novels. (David Levering Lewis: *When Harlem Was in Vogue*. New York: Knopf, 1981, Introduction.) Because Micheaux was a self-publisher and self-marketer who refused to depend on the book publishing industry with its public relations and sales efforts, his books might have escaped reviews by the publishing press and its contemporary literary critics. Later critics who have examined African American literature have either ignored him or relegated his works to an expression of the pre-Harlem Renaissance, that presented views of unrealistic accommodationism and assimilationism that appear to them to be inauthentic and out of context of the Harlem Renaissance period. (Refer to Carl Milton Hughes, *The Negro Novelist*, New York: The Citadel Press, 1953, pp. 130-132, as cited in Note #266; and Robert A. Bone, *The Negro Novel in America*, New Haven, Connecticut: Yale University Press, 1958, pp. 49-50.) Hugh M. Gloster, in his book, *Negro Voices in American Fiction*, (Chapel Hill, North Carolina: University of North Carolina Press, 1948), pp. 84-91, treats Micheaux's early work with more respect, discussing theme, plot, and narrative style of the first three books, although he admits that Micheaux's narrative style and technique are unimpressive. For whatever reason, he makes no mention of the four later books. Generally, however, there is

agreement among the critics that even at his best, Micheaux is not a polished writer and that his work does not meet their exacting creative standards.
See Note #263 for the Gehr quote. Micheaux fans, comparing notes at
the 1998 Gregory, SD, film festival, found that individuals in the group
owned the sixth and ninth editions.

[5]Carlton Moss, Filmmaker featured in *Midnight Ramble*, a Public
Broadcasting System video documentary (Northern Lights Productions for
the *American Experience*, WGBH Boston, 1994).

[6]At the Second Annual Oscar Micheaux Festival, Gregory, South
Dakota, on August 17, 1997, a series of round tables was held at which local
historians and visiting scholars discussed Micheaux, Gregory County history, and Micheaux's work. Local historian Lee Arlie Barry, who has studied
Oscar Micheaux's Gregory County experience for more than thirty years, discussed Micheaux's well-deserved reputation for castigating members of the
community with whom he disagreed, and the propensity for libel action
common among Gregory County lawyers during this period. She believes
that the lawyer who helped Micheaux prepare the novel for publication rec-
ommended that names of people and places be disguised.

[7]Interview by the writer with Harley W. Robinson, Jr., second cousin of
Oscar Micheaux, and Gloria McShann, long-time friend and confidante of
the Michaux family during their years in Great Bend, Kansas, conducted at
the Second Annual Oscar Micheaux Festival, Gregory, South Dakota, August
17, 1997.

[8]On August 18, 1996, Jack Broome, Principal of Burke High School,
Burke, South Dakota, identified all of the people and places mentioned in
The Conquest for the writer. This information can also be found in local his-
tories, one of the best of which is by Adeline S. Gnirk, *The Saga of Ponca
Land*. (Gregory, SD: Gregory *Times Advocate*, 1979), p. 19.

[9]Although Micheaux has disguised the family name as Devereaux, his
account in Chapter I of *The Conquest: The Story of a Negro Pioneer* (Lincoln,
Nebraska: Woodruff Press, 1913) provides an otherwise correct account of
his antecedents. A discussion of Micheaux's parents, along with an account
of the original spelling of the name as "Michaux", appears in several biographical sketches. The one most easily available is by Randal Woodland and
appears in the *Dictionary of Literary Biography, Volume 50: African
American Writers Before the Harlem Renaissance*. (Detroit Michigan: Gale
Research Company, 1986) pp. 108-215. Harley W. Robinson, Jr., a Micheaux
cousin, continues to use the old family name, "Michaux", which he pro-
nounces "Meeshaw", slightly accenting the first syllable. Apparently, the rest
of the family retained the original spelling, except possibly Oscar's brother,
Swan Emerson, who was known professionally by the new spelling during
his partnership with his brother. The possible French Huguenot connection

was identified by historian Herbert T. Hoover in an interview with the writer on December 1, 1997.

[10]Raines, Edgar F., Jr., "The Ku Klux Klan in Illinois, 1867-1875" *Illinois Historical Journal*, Volume 78, Number 1 (1985), pp. 17-45, p. 20.

[11]Ibid., pp. 19-24.

[12]Hodges, Carl G. and Levene, Helene H. *Illinois Negro History Makers.* (Springfield, Illinois: Illinois Emancipation Centennial Committee, State of Illinois, 1964), pp. 26-27.

[13]Carlson, Shirley J. "Black Migration to Pulaski County, Illinois: 1860-1897". *Illinois Historical Journal*, Volume 80, Number 1 (1987) pp. 37-46, p. 41.

[14]Carlson, pp. 37-46.

[15]Ibid., pp. 44-45.

[16]Suggs, Henry Lewis, Editor. *The Black Press in the Middle West.* (Westport, Connecticut: Greenwood Press, 1995.) p. 1.

[17]One of the best and most balanced discussions of conditions for black people during this period appears in the essays of W.E.B. DuBois, collected and presented in his *Souls of Black Folks*, first published in 1903. This book provides a carefully constructed rebuttal to Booker T. Washington's principles for success that DuBois felt were an oversimplification. *Souls of Black Folks* has been reprinted many times. This writer used a 1990 edition with a preface by scholar John Edgar Wideman. (New York: The Library of America, 1990.) The best study of the gradual development of "Jim Crowism" in the South is C. Vann Woodward's *The Strange Case of Jim Crow*, first published in New York by Oxford University Press in 1955 and updated by the author in 1956 and 1957.

[18]*The Conquest*, p. 13.

[19]*The Conquest*, p. 17.

[20]Gehr, Richard, "One Man Show", *American Film Magazine*, May 1991, pp. 35-38, p. 36.

[21]*The Conquest*, p. 13.

[22]Ibid., pp. 14-15.

[23]Ibid., p. 195.

[24]Micheaux. *The Homesteader*, pp. 159-173.

[25]Great Bend Historical Society, Great Bend, Kansas. This information was provided in the program for a memorial service marking Oscar Micheaux' grave, held in Great Bend, Kansas, on October 8, 1988.

[26]*The Homesteader*, p. 422.

[27]*The Conquest*, p. 17.

[28]Ibid.

[29]Interview with Harley W. Robinson, Jr., August 17, 1997.

[30]*The Conquest*, Chapter II.

[31]Ibid. Chapter II, pp. 18-25.

[32]Two excellent references tell the story of Robert Abbott and his newspaper's role in building black Chicago: Grossman, James R., "Blowing the Trumpet: The *Chicago Defender* and Black Migration During World War I", *Illinois Historical Journal*, Volume 78, Number 2, 1985, on pp. 82-96; and Walker, Juliet E.K., "The Promised Land: The *Chicago Defender* and the Black Press in Illinois: 1862-1870", in *The Black Press in the Midwest.* Edited by Suggs, Henry Lewis. Westport, Connecticut: The Greenwood Press, 1996; pp. 24-26.

[33]*The Conquest*, Chapters II and III. Also summarized by Fontenot, Chester J., Jr., "Oscar Micheaux, Black Novelist and Film Maker", in *Vision and Refuge: Essays on the Literature of the Great Plains*, Lincoln, Nebraska: University of Nebraska Press, 1982. pp.109-125; pp.112-113.

[34]*The Conquest*, pp. 70-71; *The Wind from Nowhere*, p. 55., *The Forged Note*, pp. 65-68, p. 166.

[35]Williamson, Joel. *A Rage for Order: Black/White Relations in the American South Since Emancipation.* (New York: Oxford University Press, 1986), pp. 65-67.

[36]Young, Joseph I., *Oscar Micheaux's Novels: Black Apologies for White Oppression.* Unpublished dissertation. (Lincoln, Nebraska: University of Nebraska, 1984.) p. 45.

[37]*The Conquest*, Chapters IV and V.

[38]Santino, Jack. *Miles of Smiles, Years of Struggle: Stories of Black Pullman Porters.* (Urbana, Illinois: University of Illinois Press, 1989.) Chapter 1.

[39]Ibid.

[40]Ibid.

[41]Ibid.

[42]*The Conquest*, Chapter V and VII. Micheaux describes life on the road from an insider's point of view. For an additional scholarly account of the Pullman porters and their struggle for labor equality, refer to William H. Harris, *Keeping the Faith.* (Urbana, Illinois: University of Illinois Press, 1977.)

[43]Santino, 71.

[44]Ibid., 90-96.

[45]*The Conquest*, pp. 44-45, and pp. 58-59. In the latter reference, Micheaux describes how he returned to portering by staying away from the Chicago Western Division of Pullman and registering for work from the St. Louis office.

[46]Ibid. pp. 42-43.

[47]Ibid, pp. 42-45.

[48]Ibid., p. 54. In choosing his disguised names for this account of his homesteading experience, Micheaux resorted to easily translatable cognomens. He referred to the Rosebud as the Little Crow because, as he said, it was the name of an Indian chief currently residing in the area [and also a

Day School near Carter]. Interestingly, when Micheaux reworked the home-steading material in his other novels, he identified all of the place names correctly.

[49]Ibid., p. 94.

[50]Throughout this chapter, the reader will encounter various terms describing the Indian population on the Great Sioux Reservation. We turn for clarification to a 1996 interview with Herbert T. Hoover, Ph.D., profes-sor of upper midwestern history and expert on the Sioux peoples: This large nation of plains Indians settled first in central and northern Minnesota and southern Canada but were pushed westward by their old enemies, the Ojibwa or Chippewa, when the French and English occupied traditional Ojibwa lands. Most of the Sioux nation left Minnesota and began ranging on horseback over the Great Plains where they led nomadic lives pursuing the buffalo, and securing agricultural staples from the Arikara (Rees) and Mandans, agrarian tribes living in the area. Here they also developed cor-dial relations and military alliances with the Cheyenne. The name "Sioux" is not the name they gave themselves, but was a pejorative, meaning "Snake," given them by their Ojibwa enemies and picked up by the whites. Over the years it permanently attached itself to these people who have adopted it as a convenient, if inaccurate, way to refer to themselves. Today the term "Lakota" is used by whites and some Indians in an attempt to be more accu-rate, but this designation is also problematic for the purist and for tradition-al Indians, since it refers only to the westernmost nation. The Sioux people actually consist of three nations, with a total of 14 clearly defined "bands". The three major nations, Lakota, Nakota, and Dakota, are characterized by slight linguistic differences. The Lakota, originally designated the "Teton Sioux" by white explorers, comprise the largest and westernmost nation, and also, historically, were confirmed "separatists" and remained the most unwilling to submit to the American military. Within this nation are found the following bands: Oglala, Hunkpapa, Two Kettle, Sans Arc, Upper and Lower Brule, Minneconjou, and Blackfoot Sioux. The Nakota originally occupied the central portion of "Sioux Country", and consisted of the Yanktonais and the peaceful Yanktons. The "Eastern Sioux" or Dakota bands, known as the Sisseton-Wahpeton and the Mdewankaton-Wahpekute remained in central Minnesota and northeastern South Dakota, and portions of the band known as "Santee" were forcibly removed to an inhospitable reservation in central South Dakota, and later to a small reservation in north-eastern Nebraska, after some of their men took part part in the bloody Minnesota Sioux Wars in 1862. During Micheaux's time and continuing today, the term "Rosebud Sioux" is often used among Indians as well as whites to refer to Native Americans living on the Rosebud Reservation, but as described in Notes 53-55, the Rosebud has been occupied from the begin-ning by an "international" collection of Sioux people representing many, if not all, of the various bands.

[51]Jorgenson, Gladys White, *Before the Homesteads in Tripp County and the Rosebud*. (Freeman, South Dakota: Pine Hill Press, 1974) p. 12, and Chambers, Opie, "The Early History of the Rosebud Country," *Gregory Times Advocate* in *A Rosebud Review*, 1913, July 1984, pp. 5-9. The latter is a reprint of a supplement to the Burke *Gazette* originally published for its readers in 1913.

[52]See Note #50.

[53]Readers with curiosity about how Gregory became a place opened to settlement will be interested in this information. Rosebud Agency took shape at its permanent location in 1878, without specific jurisdictional boundaries on the Great Sioux Reservation. Rosebud Reservation appeared under authority from the Sioux Agreement of 1889 as the largest ever established in Sioux Country, comprising 3,228,161 acres spread over five counties in southwestern South Dakota.

For more than a decade, the Rosebud census remained in a state of flux. In 1886, it was reported at 7,656, but by 1892 it dropped to 4,254. The decline resulted partly from voluntary movement by groups among the six new Lakota and Yanktonai reservations. In addition, more than 600 from the Rosebud jurisdiction were taken as prisoners of war after Wounded Knee, and involuntarily enrolled at Pine Ridge, while others made the move voluntarily. Rosebud lost as many as 900 this way, but in 1898 added 442 Lower Brules in the Big White River District.

Thereafter the census became more stable—at 4,917 in 1901, and at 5,516 by 1923. Approximately 5,000 reservation residents owned in common some 645 acres per capita.

After the year 1900, they began to accept allotments, and they leased as many as 49 scattered, tribally-owned "pastures" to outside cattlemen for cash. In 1901, U.S. Inspector James McLaughlin persuaded them to sell acreages left over after allotment for funds to help with adjustments to family farming and ranching, and to elevate the value of their new allotments as real estate through regional economic growth.

They assented to three land sales: one in Gregory County, authorized by an act of Congress dated April 23, 1904 (33 *Stat.*, 254); one in Tripp County, authorized on March 2, 1907 (34 *Stat.*, 1229); another in Mellette and Washabaugh counties thereafter.

On September 14, 1901, an agreement to sell 416,000 acres in Gregory County at $2.50 per acre (twice the amount charged by the United States for most public land) bore the signatures or marks of 1,031 voting adults. [Council with Rosebud by Inspector James McLaughlin, April 13, McLaughlin to Secretary of the Interior, October 5, 1901, Irregular Sized Papers, #106, National Archives.] Gregory County contained 521,050.24 acres, of which Indian residents had taken 104,909 with the best agricultural qualities in 452 allotments. Officials reserved small acreages for missions, a school, and a sub-agency to assure the continuation of federal services.

A report for the year 1921 indicated this disposition of payment received for 416,000 acres: The total paid in annual per capita amounts through the years 1905-1913 was $1,285,437.19. The balance in an interest bearing account in 1921 was $6,232.81. [Assistant Commissioner E.B. Merritt to Mr. Buffalo Bear, April 6, 1922, Indian Central Classified File, #211, National Archives.]

By December 31, 1910, a similar sale in Tripp County placed in two interest-bearing accounts a total of $1,198,460.16. From this amount, $1,000,000 went into an account for use in per capita payments. [Acting Indian Commissioner to Secretary of the Interior, April 11, 1907, Letters Received by the Office of Indian Affairs, Second Assistant Commissioner C.F. Hauke to Superintendent John B. Woods, March 30, 1911, Indian Central Classified File #220, National Archives.]

The Mellette-Washabaugh land opening was similar to these. The land rush that brought Oscar Micheaux to Gregory County came through the exercise of persuasive pressure by Inspector McLaughlin and the Rosebud Superintendent, to be sure, but it took place with approval by most adults in search of funds to develop farms and ranches on allotments.

[54]Federal Indian policy during those years was based on a belief that the only way to achieve peace with the Indians was to destroy tribal identities to the greatest possible extent. One way that this was achieved was to move groups of Indians around within the reservation system without regard to tribal identity. Thus, Sioux people were mixed on the reservations regardless of their "national or band" identity, and sometimes "surplus" Indians from other tribes were placed on reservations where land was available. Naturally, intermarriage among the bands and/or tribes occurred, as did marriages between whites and Indians. Federal agents responsible for administering Indian policy on the Rosebud might have considered the international and accomodationist flavor on this reservation to be a measure of the success of those policies, since tribal identities were blurred and it appeared that many of the accommodationist Indians were achieving a level of success at adapting to white ways. It was not until the late 1920s that an extensive government survey, intended to measure the success of accommodationism, revealed it as failed policy. While changes in policy were made immediately and implemented gradually and inconsistently, the current policy that encourages tribes and bands to return to their tribal identity was not implemented consistently until the social movements of the Great Society in the 1960s provided empowerment, training, and capital to enable the tribes to begin to achieve self-determination.

[55]Annual Reports, August 29, 1869, August 29, 1870, Spotted Tail Agency, National Archives - Kansas City; Special Commissioners Edward C. Kimball and Henry E. Alvord to Commissioner of Indian Affairs, June 16, 1873, M234, roll 252, National Archives; "Background Data on Indians at the

Rosebud Reservation," October 1, 1953, Record Group 75, Accession No. 57A457, Box 63085, National Archives - Denver.

[56]Jorgenson, pp. 44-45.

[57]The above descriptions of the Rosebud and the town of Bonesteel appear in Jorgenson's lively history, pp. 67, 49, and 45.

[58]Jackson, F. H., "Homesteading on the Rosebud," *A Rosebud Review*, 1913. Gregory, South Dakota: Gregory *Times Advocate*, July 1984, reprint of original 1913 publication. pp. 17-19.

[59]Jorgenson, p. 67.

[60]Interview with David Strain, August 3, 1998.

[61]*The Conquest*, Chapter VI.

[62]Ibid.

[63]Jorgenson, p. 67.

[64]*The Conquest*, pp. 61-62.

[65]Ibid.

[66]Ibid.

[67]Ibid. p. 64.

[68]Ibid. The complete details of Micheaux's purchase are discussed in Chapter VII, with specifics on pages 61-65. In a 1988 publication of the Gregory County Historical Society entitled, *Dallas, South Dakota: The End of the Line*, Lee Arlie Barry verified the legal description from the Gregory County Records, Book RM, page 29, for Micheaux's first homestead, corroborating the data provided in *The Conquest*. The property was in Rhodes Township.

[69]*The Conquest*, Chapter VII.

[70]Ibid, pp. 70-71.

[71]*The Conquest*, Chapters IX and X; quoted material appears on p.74.

[72]Jorgenson, pp. 64-79.

[73]With the revived interest in Micheaux, and the Annual Micheaux Film Festival in Gregory County, SD, a variety of local information is surfacing, much of which will require future examination by scholars to determine its validity. Some of the material has been filtered through two or more generations of family oral history and cannot be accurately verified. Some material is unflattering and demeaning and must be considered in light of the general cultural misunderstanding and racial bigotry common to this historical period. Most is presented without complete access to his writings or to the research of other Micheaux scholars. Other valuable and well-researched material is still in the possession of local scholars and historians. When all becomes available, the entire body will represent an important contribution to Micheaux literature. Because of the need for further careful examination of this material, I have made the conscious choice to exclude most of it from this study. The Gregory County Oscar Micheaux Society continues to gather material in connection with the annual festival and hopes someday to

become the official repository of Micheaux papers and a center for scholarly research.

[74]University of South Dakota Oral History Library. Interview #871 by Steve Plummer on July 27, 1973, with Dick Siler, Rosebud pioneer, homesteader, and Micheaux neighbor.

[75]Some of these incidents are recounted in the county histories, including *The Saga of Ponca Land*, and in oral accounts at the University of South Dakota's Oral History Library. Others were told at the First Annual Oscar Micheaux Film Festival, held August 17-19, 1996, in Gregory, and at the Second Annual Film Festival held on the same dates in 1997.

[76]Hebert, Janis, "Oscar Micheaux, A Black Pioneer", *South Dakota Review*, 10, Winter 1973, 63-69. p. 64. Hebert cites correspondence by Don Coonen with University of South Dakota professor John Milton that repeated a prevailing local view that Micheaux's railroad experience gave him an inside track with respect to the future route of the railroad. As "Micheaux fever" grips the Rosebud in the wake of national attention derived from the annual festival, and as the old ones pass on, it will be increasingly difficult to verify the accuracy of many of these stories.

[77]*The Conquest*, pp. 77-78.

[78]*The Conquest*, p. 80.

[79]Paula M. Nelson. *After the West Was Won: Homesteaders and Town-Builders in Western South Dakota, 1900-1917.* (Iowa City, Iowa: University of Iowa Press, 1986.) pp. 51-52, 127-128.

[80]*The Conquest*, Chapters X and XI.

[81]Hebert, p. 62. Note: South Dakota critics who farmed in the upper Great Plains appear to have forgotten that Micheaux was the son and grandson of successful farmers in the upper south. Interviews with farmers familiar with techniques used in the early days in southern Arkansas, Missouri, and Illinois suggest that Micheaux may have been attempting to use a technique that worked well in warmer latitudes.

[82]*The Conquest*, pp. 77-78.

[83]Ibid.

[84]Ibid, pp. 92-93.

[85]The *Chicago Defender*, March 19, 1910, and later reprinted in *The Conquest* as Chapter XXIII.

[86]DuBois, Chapters VI-VIII.

[87]*The Conquest*, pp. 117-118. Micheaux told the story of the Gregory-Dallas competition in detail in Chapters XV-XIX.

[88]*A Rosebud Review*, 1913. pp. 69-80. In this lengthy booster article written in 1913, the history of "Old Dallas" and the fight with Gregory that resulted in its relocation to "New" Dallas is not addressed. Instead, the article cites the beginning of the town as April 20, 1907, in time for the Tripp County boom. The town as it exists today is known simply as "Dallas".

162   Oscar Micheaux

⁸⁹*The Conquest*, pp. 120-122.

⁹⁰*The Conquest*, p. 147.

⁹¹Winner Chamber of Commerce, *Tripp County, South Dakota, 1909-1984 Diamond Jubilee*. (Freeman, South Dakota: Pine Hill Press, 1984) p. 24.

⁹²Bowser, Pearl and Spence, Louise, "Identity and Betrayal: *The Symbol of the Unconquered* and Oscar Micheaux's "Biographical Legend", in *The Birth of Whiteness*, edited by Daniel Bernardi. (New Brunswick, New Jersey: Rutgers University Press, 1996.) pp. 56-75, p. 61.

⁹³*Tripp County, South Dakota 1909-1984, Diamond Jubilee*, pp. 44-45.

⁹⁴Barry, *Dallas, South Dakota: The End of the Line*, p. 4.

⁹⁵VanEpps-Taylor, Betti C., *Hiding in Plain Sight: African Americans in Dakota Territory and South Dakota, 1802-1970*. A manuscript in preparation by this writer and scheduled for publication sometime in the year 2000.

⁹⁶Interview by the writer with Herbert T. Hoover, Ph.D., University of South Dakota, winter 1996.

⁹⁷Interview by the writer with Harley W. Robinson, Jr., August 18, 1997, Gregory, South Dakota.

⁹⁸*The Wind from Nowhere*, pp. 16-17.

⁹⁹Ibid, pp. 115-117. Richard Papousek, of the Gregory County Oscar Micheaux Society, provided an interesting sidebar to this material in an interview with the writer in late 1998. Related to the Vosika family mentioned in this passage, and a regular vistor to the Vosika farm just south of the original Micheaux homestead, he remembers tales of the neighborhood barn dances held in the large, old-fashioned barn that still stands. Micheaux rarely missed such entertainment, might have played an instrument in the band, and often danced with the young ladies of the neighborhood. In reconciling these accounts of Micheaux's social life, one should remember that *The Wind From Nowhere* is an autobiographical novel, a format that allows the author some license. In the above quoted passage, Micheaux was articulating the common ambivalent cultural expectations and mores indelibly etched on black America, making that point, rather than presenting a strictly factual account of his homesteading experiences. Papousek's account also suggests many South Dakotans' enduring conviction that race is mostly irrelevant so long as individuals are willing to accept and blend into the local culture.

¹⁰⁰See *The Homesteader*, pp. 148-152; also throughout *The Case of Mrs. Wingate* and *The Story of Dorothy Stanfield*.

¹⁰¹These concerns were part of the "folk knowledge" in the portions of African American society that I personally experienced as late as the 1950s and early 60s. As well, a general reading of the black newspapers and magazines of the period, especially the early issues of the *Chicago Defender*, demonstrates that these matters were frequently discussed in the press.

[102]The fact that such a law was deemed necessary indicates either that southern separatist views and the institutionalization of Jim Crowism were making themselves felt on the Great Plains, or that there was a growing trend toward legal fraternization between whites and Native Americans or blacks that would have played upon white racist fears common to the period.

[103]*The Conquest*, Chapter XXV. *The Homesteader*, Epoch II, Chapter I; *The Wind from Nowhere*, Chapter IX. See also the *Chicago Defender* microfilm for the dates 1909-1926 that frequently published news items dealing with cross-racial marriages and their consequences. These and other publications of the period provide a good reflection of prevailing attitudes among African Americans during this period. Although Micheaux enjoyed describing himself as "the only black farmer west of Omaha", obviously this was not exactly the case.

[104]See Woodward, C. Vann, *The Strange Case of Jim Crow*, previously cited, for an in-depth discussion of the development and spread of the nearly universal custom of "Jim Crow" style segregation in the post-Civil War period.

[105]*The Conquest*, Chapter XXVII, pp. 168-176.

[106]Ibid, p. 114. The apparent discrepancy in the page numbers of *The Conquest*, as identified in this and the preceding note, is an example of Micheaux's rambling narrative style. In this instance, he interrupts his story about the trials of seeking a wife with a lengthy discussion consisting of several chapters about the political aspects of "proving up" and townbuilding on the Rosebud, before returning to his pre-nuptial adventure.

[107]*The Conquest*, pp. 169-176.

[108]*The Homesteader*, Second Epoch, Chapter II. The correct name of the family of Elder N.J. McCracken and his daughter, Orlean McCracken, is found in the two *Chicago Defender* articles identified and quoted in this chapter. The name of Orlean McCracken also appears on the title of the homestead she purchased.

[109]*Chicago Defender*, April 23, 1910.

[110]Rough notes provided to the writer by Richard Papousek, Gregory County Oscar Micheaux Society, from a paper he presented at the Third Annual Oscar Micheaux Festival, August, 1998, in which he quoted this and other newspaper accounts about Oscar Micheaux. This account is from the Gregory *Times Advocate*, April 27, 1910.

[111]Papousek Paper, August, 1998. An excerpt from an article that appeared in the January 20, 1910, Gregory *Times Advocate* documents the presence of Micheaux's grandmother and sister. Entitled "Conditions in Tripp County Told", it relates the experience of a settler named Mrs. Bartels as follows: "One of Bartels' neighbors was a colorful character called Grandma Micheaux [Michaux?]. Micheaux had been a slave, was 90 years old and now lived on a homestead with her granddaughter. Her grandson,

Oscar, from Gregory would bring her supplies when he could but the prairie snows sometimes made it impossible to get there. Bartels would give her dried beans and apples when Micheaux was out of food. Micheaux was also seen every once in a while walking along with a gunny sack and a big stick. She would pick something up and put it in her sack. Later Bartels figured out that she was picking up buffalo chips to burn for fuel. When the neighbors found her without fuel they would haul a load of wood in for her. Micheaux's granddaughter [Micheaux's sister, Olivia] would come and visit Bartels. Bartels thought she was a well informed girl and loved to talk to her. The granddaughter would only come and visit when no one else was there. If someone came during her visit, she would immediately get up and leave. Bartels said, 'She seemed to fear that even though I accepted her as a friend, these other people might not'."

112*The Conquest*, beginning with Chapter XXXII and proceeding to the end of the book, details the marriage and its deterioriation.

113*The Conquest*, Chapter XXXVII, *The Homesteader*, Chapters XXV-.XXVII, *The Wind From Nowhere*, Chapters XIX through XXVIII. Lee Arlie Barry and other local historians have been unable to document the birth or death of an infant. (Interview by the writer with Mrs. Barry, August 17-19, 1996, at the First Annual Oscar Micheaux festival, Gregory, S.D.) In *The Homesteader*, Micheaux described the burial of the child on his property. The fact that its existence cannot be proven would not be unusual for the homestead period when recording of such vital statistics was sometimes carelessly done.

An interesting South Dakota sidebar to this incident occurred in *The Wind from Nowhere* on pages 235-237. Here the autobiographical protagonist, Martin Eden, and his sister (Olivia) attempted to calm his wife's relatives and remove them from the sickroom. The sister, whose homestead was near the village of Carter in Tripp County, proposed that the Chicagoans be sent to the hotel in Carter where "a Colored teacher at an Indian Day School in the next County, only about twelve miles from Carter" would visit them and make them feel at home. The teacher and his family were identified as "The Barrys." According to county histories quoted in VanEpps-Taylor's manuscript *Hiding in Plain Sight*, there were at this time two African American brothers, Solomon and Bruce Gary, living and working in the area. One, a bachelor, was a rural mail carrier; the other, who was married, was a teacher at the Little Crow Indian Day School where his wife was matron. This couple also taught Sunday School at a local church and were highly respected on the Rosebud. Two sons, Robert and Larry, were born in the 1930s, and, according to South Dakota Black Historian, Ted Blakey, the family regularly attended the annual "South Dakota Negro Picnics," statewide gatherings held at a central point each summer for more than 25 years. The Gary family later removed to Fontana, California, where the writer became acquainted with Robert and Larry who were her classmates at nearby Chaffey College in Ontario, California, from 1955-1957.

[114]*The Conquest*, Chapter XXXVII.

[115]*Chicago Defender*, April 29, 1911.

[116]*The Conquest*. Chapter XLIII.

[117]Nelson, p. 127.

[118]Ibid. Ms. Nelson is referring to Micheaux's account in *The Conquest*, Chapters XL and XLI.

[119]*The Conquest*, p. 281.

[120]Ibid, pp. 281-283.

[121]Indeed, this writer's own family was caught in that debacle. Fred C. Grow, my maternal grandfather, was editing a small town newspaper in the burgeoning homesteading area around Hoven, near the Sully County Colored Colony east of Pierre, where the same over-speculation phenomenon had occurred. His livelihood depended on the publication of the legal notices required of all homesteaders as part of "proving up". When the drought forced many homesteaders into abandoning their lands, Grow was driven to near bankruptcy and, in desperation, moved his large and ever-expanding family to a more secure future in Watertown, close to the eastern boundary of the state. It took them many years of hard work to recover from the financial ruin they had faced.

[122]*The Conquest*, Chapters XLI and XLII.

[123]Ibid.

[124]Micheaux tells this story in detail in *The Homesteader*, pages 401-404; the quoted material appears on pages 401-402.

[125]Ibid., p. 402.

[126]The Gregory County Oscar Micheaux Society owns a copy of *The Conquest* containing a penciled notation which identifies Chapter XV as having been ghosted for Micheaux by this attorney.

[127]Paper, Papousek, August, 1998, quoting the *Dallas News*, December 12, 1912.

[128]Paper, Papousek, August, 1998, quoting the Gregory *Times Advocate*, March 20, 1913.

[129]*The Homesteader*, Chapter VI.

[130]Paper, Papousek, August, 1998, quoting the Gregory *Times Advocate*, April 3, 1913.

[131]*The Homesteader*, Chapter VI.

[132]Sampson, Henry T., *Blacks in Black and White, A Source Book on Black Films*. (Metuchen, New Jersey: The Scarecrow Press, 1977) p. 44.

[133]Paper, Papousek, August, 1998, quoting the Gregory *Times Advocate* in the above-dated article.

[134]*The Conquest*, pp. 407-411. The exact terms of Micheaux's deal with the printer will probably never be known. They are reproduced here as they

appear in *The Homesteader*. Over his life, he repeatedly reworked the story of how he became a self-publisher, and each time the specifics vary, although the gist of it remains the same and is probably substantially accurate. For example, his last version of the autobiography, *The Wind From Nowhere*, was set sometime after 1920. In this account, the protagonist, Martin Eden, also wrote of his experiences in an attempt to recoup losses from depression and drought as well his perfidious marriage. This account is substantially the same except for dollar and sales figures which Micheaux may have revised to reflect changing economic times — or he may have simply changed them for other reasons.

[135]*The Forged Note*, pp. 25, 131, 171, 185.

[136]Ibid, p. 411.

[137]Paper, Papousek, August, 1998, quoting the Gregory *Times Advocate*, July 31, 1913.

[138]A "first edition" of *The Forged Note* indicated its place of publishing to be Lincoln, Nebraska; Western Book & Supply Company, 1915. This edition featured unusual "pen and ink" illustrations of people and excerpts from the text, and Micheaux's forward "To One Whose Name Does Not Appear", showed "New Orleans, La. August 1, 1915". Also on the frontispiece of this edition was the statement, "Press of the Woodruff Bank Note Co., Lincoln, Nebr." Later editions emanated from his Sioux City offices.

[139]E. Franklin Frazier was an African American sociologist trained by Charles Spurgeon Johnson, a pioneer black sociologist from the University of Chicago. Frazier's landmark study, cited in Note #2, marked the first serious attempt to study and describe the emerging black middle class with all of its various contradictions.

[140]Lewis, David Levering, *When Harlem Was In Vogue*. (New York: Alfred A. Knopf, 1981) This well-researched and highly readable discussion of Harlem and the so-called Harlem Renaissance provides outstanding insights into the African American cultural explosion that began in Harlem after World War I and dwindled in the wake of the Great Depression. In this study, Lewis writes engagingly about how key black intellectuals and social engineers conceived and publicized the concept of the "Harlem Renaissance", structuring it to present artistic and creative work that would meet the exacting standards expected by a supercritical and doubting white artistic world. These African American leaders included Frazier, Charles Spurgeon Johnson, W.E.B. DuBois, also a trained sociologist, James Weldon Johnson and his brother, Rosamond, Walter White, who would later head the NAACP, Jessie Fausset, Alain Locke and others. Also participating in creating the movement were sympathetic, well-placed white intellectuals, including the Spingarn brothers and Mary White Ovington. Artists whose work was spotlighted in the Harlem Renaissance included Zora Neale Hurston, Langston Hughes, Countee Cullen, Nella Larsen, and many others. Micheaux's work was pointedly ignored, a slight that he never forgave.

[141]Micheaux, *The Forged Note*, Chapters III and V.

[142]Ibid. Book One, Chapter XVII.

[143]*Chicago Defender.* Throughout the months of December, 1910, and January-February, 1911, this newspaper continually covered the results of the Y's fund raising campaign, often acidly commenting editorially and by cartoon on the considerable hardship such fund raising created for already hard-pressed black workers and business people, and contrasting that struggle with the ease of white philanthropists who simply wrote checks on their millions.

[144]Woodland, p. 220.

[145]Letter from Don G. Coonen to Dr. John Milton, professor of English, University of South Dakota, written sometime in early 1971 and a part of Dr. Milton's papers which now reside at the Center for Western Studies, Augustana College, Sioux Falls, South Dakota. See Note #76. Mr. Coonen, who lived briefly on the farm that Micheaux had occupied, was researching the legal description of Micheaux's farm for Dr. Milton and stated, "A Mrs. George Liegel [working at the Register of Deeds office] ...told me that Micheaux did rent the farm where I live for a time. Where I live there is a house just across the road. This is where her father & father's brother's [sic] lived neighbors. Her uncle went in the army and Micheaux rented the place."

[146]Paper, Papousek, August, 1998, quoting the *Colome Times,* September 15, 1915.

[147]Observation made at the Roundtable Discussion, Second Annual Oscar Micheaux Festival, August 17, 1997, and supported in a subsequent interview with regional historian Herbert T. Hoover.

[148]Later, Chicago, Milwaukee, St. Paul and Pacific Railroad.

[149]Polk's City Directory for 1917, Introductory Material.

[150]Polk's City Directory for 1917, pp. 333-334. The write notes the apparent discrepancies in abbreviations used in the directory. For example, "rooms" is sometimes abbreviated as "r" and sometimes as "rms." These discrepancies appear without explanation.

[151]Polk's City Directory for 1917. Anthony is listed on page 80; the Dalhays appear on page 153.

[152]Polk's City Directory 1917 lists the physician as "c;" in the same publication for 1918 the "c" is removed.

[153]Polk's City Directories, prepared annually, always identified the churches, ministers, and current membership estimates. Malone AME Church was the older of the two institutions, established in 1886; Mt. Zion Baptist came along in 1901. Depending on which year's directory is consulted, membership during this period fluctuated, but probably the churches reached many black citizens who might not have been official members.

[154]Ibid.

[155]Interview in August, 1996, in Yankton, South Dakota, with Ted Blakey, South Dakota State Black Historian and recognized authority on black families which settled in Yankton and later migrated to Sioux City.

[156]Polk's City Directory, 1918, p. 334.

[157]Micheaux, Oscar. *The Wind from Nowhere*, New York: Book Supply Company, 1941, Dedication.

[158]Micheaux, *The Forged Note*, Lincoln, Nebraska: Western Book and Supply Company, 1915, front matter.

[159]Polk's City Directory for 1918, p. 596.

[160]Polk's Directory 1917, p. 504.

[161]It is interesting to drive the streets of West Sioux City in 1998 and remember Oscar Micheaux's brief sojourn in the city. Few of the old buildings on 7th Street can be distinguished; most have been torn down and replaced with modern structures or remodeled beyond recognition. However, the Palace Theater still stands. It must have been a modest building even in its day; today it is a vacant nondescript asphalt-shingled narrow storefront next to the modern Kollman Appliance Company and across the street from Saigon Video and a new Rent-to-Own store. Modern 7th Street features an up-to-date Salvation Army headquarters complete with store, meeting rooms and soup kitchen. Nearby are the Goodwill and Junior League resale shops, auto parts houses, bars, buildings housing light industry, and an occasional ramshackle ethnic restaurant, Mexican or Vietnamese, reflecting the changed neighborhood. The area west of 7th has undergone major renovation and boasts well-kept low income housing, grassy parks, and an old elementary school that is now the home of the Lamb Theater, a semi-professional community theater that presents a well-rounded schedule of live theater presentations and includes a program for young actors. On 6th Street, between the two blocks where Micheaux briefly lived, elderly resident Marvin English talked to me about the many changes in the neighborhood, remarking that it had always been a well-integrated neighborhood with few racial tensions despite the modest resources of many of the residents.

[162]*Chicago Defender*, 1909-1911.

[163]Paper, Papousek, August 1998, quoting the Gregory *Times Advocate*, April 11, 1918.

[164]Cripps, Thomas, *Slow Fade to Black: The Negro in American Film, 1900-1942.* (New York: Oxford University Press, 1977), Chapter One.

[165]Ibid.

[166]*Midnight Ramble*, video. See Note #4.

[167]Rhines, Jesse Algernon. *Black Film White Money.* (New Brunswick, New Jersey: Rutgers University Press, 1996.) p. 15.

[168]Cripps, Chapter One.

[169]Reid, Mark A. *Redefining Black Film*. (Los Angeles, California: University of California Press, 1993) Chapter 1, pp. 8-9.

[170]Cripps, Chapter Two.

[171]Ibid.

[172]Ibid.

[173]Ibid, p. 82.

[174]Reid, Chapter 1.

[175]Cripps, pp. 184-185.

[176]Ibid.

[177]Ibid.

[178]Ibid.

[179]*Chicago Defender*, Theater Section, February 22, 1919.

[180]*Chicago Defender* Theater Section, March 1, 1919.

[181]Ibid.

[182]*Chicago Defender* Theater Section, March through July, 1919.

[183]Second Annual Oscar Micheaux Festival, Gregory, S.D., August, 1997. This community festival honoring one of its most famous citizens makes much of the fact that *The Homesteader* was shown at its local theater soon after it was released.

[184]Cripps, p. 185.

[185]*Midnight Ramble*. See Note #5.

[186]Waskow, Arthur I., *From Race Riot to Sit-In, 1919 and the 1960s*. (Garden City, New York: Doubleday and Company, Inc., 1965) pp. 1-3.

[187]Ibid., Chapter III.

[188]Ibid.

[189]Ibid., Chapter IV.

[190]Ibid.

[191]Waskow, Appendix B. Excerpts are "verbatim reproductions of posters, notices, and throwaways published in the Chicago Negro community in the aftermath of the 1919 riot... All are from NAACP MSS." (p.308)

[192]Ibid.

[193]*The Forged Note*, p. 97.

[194]*Chicago Defender*, January 10, 1920.

[195]Sampson, pp. 44-45.

[196]Cripps, p. 186.

[197]Sampson, p. 47.

[198]*Chicago Defender*, Theater Section, January 31, 1920.

[199]Cripps, pp. 185-186.

[200]*Chicago Defender*, "News about Town", January 31, 1920. This writer has been unable to locate any trace of a book or film with the title, *The Brand of Cain*.

[201]*Chicago Defender*, July 10, 1920.

[202]Cripps, p. 186.
[203]*Chicago Defender*, April 10, 1920.
[204]*Chicago Defender*, May 29, 1920.
[205]Cripps, p. 186.
[206]*Chicago Defender*, September 28, 1920.
[207]*Chicago Defender*, Theater section, January 8, 1921.
[208]Bowser and Spence, p. 61.
[209]Ibid. Also, Sampson, pp. 97-98.
[210]Bowser & Spence, p. 65.
[211]Bowser and Spence, p. 69, quoting a review that appeared in the January-February, 1921, issue.
[212]Ibid. Bowser and Spence identified their source as quoted in *The New York Age*, 10/06/09.
[213]Ibid.
[214]Sampson, 45.
[215]*Chicago Defender*, September 4, 1920.
[216]Cripps, pp. 188-189.
[217]Ibid.
[218]Ibid.
[219]Ibid.
[220]Ibid.
[221]Charlene Regester, "Oscar Micheaux the Entrepreneur: Financing *The House Behind the Cedars*", *Journal of Film and Video*, Vol. 49.1-2, (Spring-Summer 1997.) pp. 17-27, p. 18.
[222]Ibid., p. 19.
[223]Sampson, p. 11.
[224]Regester, p. 23.
[225]Ibid., p. 19.
[226]Ibid, p. 19-20.
[227]*Chicago Defender*, July 8, 1922, quoted in Sampson, p. 48.
[228]DeLeighbur, Don. "Stardom for Negroes Only" *Philadelphia Tribune*, September 16, 1944. Reprinted in *Negro Digest*, Volume III, No. 1, November, 1944, pp. 87-88.
[229]*Chicago Defender*, January 31, 1925, quoted in Sampson, pp. 48-49.
[230]Ibid.
[231]Sampson, p. 5.
[232]Bogle, Donald. *Toms, Coons, Mulattoes, Mammies and Bucks: An Interpretive History of Blacks in American Films.* (New Expanded Edition) (New York: Continuum, 1990.) p. 111.
[233]Ibid.
[234]Ibid.
[235]Ibid.

[236]Cripps, p. 186.

[237]Ibid., pp. 187-188.

[238]Ibid., 190-191.

[239]Ibid., p. 191.

[240]Sampson, Chapter 6.

[241]Barry, p. 7.

[242]Sampson, p. 49.

[243]Sampson, p. 50.

[244]Ibid.

[245]Interview by the writer with Harley W. Robinson, Jr., August, 1997.

[246]Reid, pp. 14-17.

[247]Ibid., pp. 16-17.

[248]Sampson, p. 51.

[249]Sampson, p. 51.

[250]Bowser and Spence, Note #71, p. 79.

[251]Reid, p. 15. One of the best sources for information about black actors and actresses who worked with Micheaux is Sampson's *Blacks in Black and White*, previously cited. The book provides basic biographical information for many of these people and, in some cases, adds unique personalized information. On pages 250-252, Sampson reproduces excerpts from three articles which appeared in the *Pittsburgh Courier* on June 11, 18, and 25, 1927, in which Miss Preer describes what it was like to make pictures with Oscar Micheaux.

[252]Sampson, pp. 250-252; Reid, pp. 15-16.

[253]Reid, p. 16.

[254]Sampson, pp. 146-47.

[255]Larsen, Nella. *Quicksand*, (New York: Knopf, 1928); and *Passing*, (New York: Knopf, 1929). Fausset, Jessie, *Plum Bun*, (New York: Knopf, 1929).

[256]Sampson, p. 53.

[257]Cripps, p. 343.

[258]Sampson, p. 53; Cripps, pp. 343-345.

[259]*The Case of Mrs. Wingate*, Chapter III.

[260]Sioux Falls *Argus Leader*, Sioux Falls, South Dakota, March 4, 1940, as quoted by Strain, David, in his 1997 paper, "Oscar Micheaux, South Dakota's Most Famous Pioneer," *Fifth Annual West River History Conference Papers from September 18, 19, & 20, 1997 West River History Conference*, sponsored by the Keystone Area Historical Society, Keystone, South Dakota 57751, pp. 430-438, p. 433.

[261]Bowser and Spence, p. 57.

[262]*The Case of Mrs. Wingate*, pp. 74-75

[263]Gehr, Richard, p. 38.

[264]Lewis, David Levering, Introduction.

[265]In all of his novels, the reader views slices of black life, ranging from the ghettos of the Teens in Cincinnati, Atlanta, Birmingham, Memphis, and New Orleans in *The Forged Note*, to the homesteader's visits during different time periods to Chicago and Harlem in *The Conquest, The Homesteader*, and *The Wind from Nowhere*. In the two murder mysteries, the reader views black life in New York City, Chicago, Memphis, and Atlanta during the Thirties and Forties.

[266]Hughes, Carl Milton. *The Negro Novelist, A Discussion of the Writings of American Negro Novelists, 1940-1950*. (New York: The Citadel Press, 1953) pp. 132-133. Critic Hughes described this novel as follows: "He cannot rid himself of the idea of a scenario writer, and his books always bear the mark of sensationalism. His most recent books show the influence of pulp and detective periodicals. He attempts to be a serious writer, but he hardly has creative imagination and misses the reality of things by his theatrical posturing. His indictment of the Jews as usurpers of the Negro film industry apparently does not have sufficient evidence to support it. Immediately one becomes a little skeptical about the issues and themes his books purport to develop. In effect, he seems to say that Georgia white women crave Negro men, and there were black Germans interested in the cause of Nazism in the United States... The fact that Kent, a character in *Mrs. Wingate*, has to apprehend a Negro criminal winks at plausibility...".

[267]*Chicago Defender*, January 9, 1926.

[268]Bowser and Spence, Notes, p.79.

[269]The *Chicago Defender*, from 1905 well into the 1920s, featured regular advertisements for the black-owned Binga Bank, owned by a male African American businessman named Jesse Binga.

[270]Several critics have commented on this unfortunate choice of subject. See Hughes, p. 131. This critic dismisses *The Masquerade* out of hand as "a distinct failure. A novelist is always on dangerous grounds when he essays to write another novelist's successfully wrought novel."

[271]*The Story of Dorothy Stanfield*, Chapter 5, and pp. 305-308.

[272]Rampersad, Arnold. *The Life of Langston Hughes: Volume 1, 1902-1941, I Too Sing America*. (New York: Oxford University Press, 1986) Chapter 7.

[273]My manuscript, *Hiding in Plain Sight: The African American Experience in Dakota Territory and South Dakota, 1802-1970*, describes several such families: the Blairs, McGruders, and Speeces of Sully County, the Baileys of rural Edgemont, the Blakeys of Yankton, the Warrens and Mahones of Huron, and the Mitchells of Sioux Falls, among others.

[274]Woodland, p. 224, quoting Oscar Micheaux.

[275]Cripps, Thomas. *Making Movies Black: The Hollywood Message Movie from World War II to the Civil Rights Era*. (New York: Oxford University Press, 1993) pp. 36, 104.

[276]Cripps, p. 146.

[277]Ibid.

[278]Ibid.

[279]Ibid.

[280]This is standard biographical information and appears in virtually all sources.

[281]Interview by the writer with Harley W. Robinson, Jr., August 17, 1997.

[282]Strain, David, p. 443, quoting the *Ebony* article.

[283]Ibid, p. 435. Strain is quoting the Sioux Falls *Argus Leader* article dated February 21, 1989.

[284]Ibid, p. 434.

[285]See Note #5.

[286]Ibid, 434.

[287]Smalley, Columbus. "Oscar Micheaux", in *The Black 100: A Ranking of the Most Influential African Americans, Past and Present*, (New York: Carol Publishing Group, 1993), pp. 293-296, p. 293.

[288]Quoted from Sampson, pp. 55-56.

BIBLIOGRAPHY
Books

Bogle, Donald. *Toms, Coons, Mulattoes, Mammies, & Bucks: An Interpretive History of Blacks in American Films.* New York: The Continuum Publishing Company, 1990.

Bone, Robert A. *The Negro Novelist in America.* New Haven, Connecticut: Yale University Press, 1958.

Coursey, O.W. *Literature of South Dakota.* Mitchell, South Dakota: The Educator Supply Company, 1916.

Cripps, Thomas. *Making Movies Black: The Hollywood Message Movie from World War II to the Civil Rights Era.* New York: Oxford University Press, 1993.

____. *Slow Fade to Black: The Negro in American Film.* New York: Oxford University Press, 1977.

DuBois, W.E.B. *Souls of Black Folks.* New York: The Library of America, 1990.

Fausset, Jessie. *Plum Bun.* New York: Alfred A. Knopf, 1929.

Frazier, E. Franklin. *Black Bourgeoisie: The Rise of A New Middle Class.* New York: The Free Press, 1957.

Gloster, Hugh M. *Negro Voices in American Fiction.* Chapel Hill, North Carolina: University of North Carolina Press, 1948.

Gnirk, Adeline S. *The Saga of Ponca Land.* Gregory, South Dakota: Gregory *Times Advocate*, 1979.

Gregory County Historical Society. *Dallas, South Dakota, The End of the Line.* Gregory, South Dakota: Gregory *Times Advocate*, 1988. (Previously printed in 1971)

Harris, William H., *Keeping the Faith: A. Philip Randolph and Milton P. Webster and the Brotherhood of Sleeping Car Porters, 1925-27.* Urbana, Illinois: University of Illinois Press, 1977.

Higgins, Nathan Irvin. *Harlem Renaissance.* New York: Oxford University Press, 1971.

Hodges, Carl G. and Levene, Helene M. *Illinois Negro History Makers.* Springfield, Illinois: Illinois Emancipation Centennial Committee, State of Illinois, 1964.

Hughes, Carl Milton. *The Negro Novelist: A Discussion of The Writings of American Negro Novelists, 1940-1950.* New York: The Citadel Press, 1953.

Jones, G. William. *Black Cinema Treasures, Lost and Found.* Denton, Texas: University of Texas Press, 1991.

Jorgenson, Gladys White. *Before the Homesteads in Tripp County and the Rosebud.* Freeman, South Dakota: Pine Hill Press, 1974

Larsen, Nella. *Passing.* New York: Alfred A. Knopf, 1929.

_____. *Quicksand.* New York: Alfred A. Knopf, 1928.

Leab, Daniel J. *From Sambo to Superspade.* Boston, Massachusetts: Houghton Miflin Company, 1976.

Lewis, David Levering. *When Harlem Was In Vogue.* New York: Alfred A. Knopf, 1981.

Micheaux, Oscar. *The Conquest: The Story of a Negro Pioneer by the Pioneer.* Lincoln, Nebraska: Woodruff, 1913, reprint: Lincoln, Nebraska: University of Nebraska Press, 1994.

_____. *The Forged Note: A Romance of the Darker Races.* Lincoln Nebraska: Western Book Supply Company, 1915.

_____. *The Homesteader.* Sioux City, Iowa: Western Book Supply 1917, reprint: Lincoln, Nebraska: University of Nebraska Press, 1994.

_____. *The Wind from Nowhere.* New York: New York Book Supply, 1944.

_____. *The Case of Mrs. Wingate.* New York: New York Book Supply, 1945.

_____. *The Story of Dorothy Stanfield, Based on a Great Insurance Swindle and a Woman.* New York: New York Book Supply, 1946.

_____. *The Masquerade: An Historical Romance.* New York: New York Book Supply, 1947.

Nelson, Paula M. *After the West Was Won: Homesteaders and Town Builders in Western South Dakota, 1900-1917.* Iowa City, Iowa: University of Iowa Press, 1986.

Polk's City Directory, Sioux City Iowa. 1917. Sioux City, Iowa: R.L. Polk and Company, Publishers, 514-516 United Bank Building, Sioux City, Iowa.

Polk's City Directory, Sioux City, Iowa, 1918. Sioux City, Iowa: R.L. Polk and Company, Publishers, 514-516 United Bank Building, Sioux City, Iowa.

Rampersad, Arnold. *The Life of Langston Hughes, Volume 1, 1902-1941. I Too Sing America.* New York: Oxford University Press, 1986.

Reid, Mark A. *Redefining Black Film.* Los Angeles, California: University of California Press, 1993.

Rhines, Jesse Algernon. *Black Film, White Money.* New Brunswick, New Jersey: Rutgers University Press, 1996.

Salley, Columbus. *The Black 100: A Ranking of the 100 Most Influential Black Americans, Past and Present.* New York: Carol Publishing Group, 1993.

Sampson, Henry T. *Blacks in Black and White: A Source Book on Black Films.* Metuchen, New Jersey: The Scarecrow Press, 1977.

Santino, Jack. *Miles of Smiles, Years of Struggle: Stories of Black Pullman Porters.* Urbana, Illinois: University of Illinois Press, 1989.

Suggs, Henry Lewis. *The Black Press in the Middle West.* Westport, Connecticut: The Greenwood Press, 1996.

Waskow, Arthur I. *From Race Riot to Sit-In, 1919 and the 1960s.* Garden City, New York: Doubleday and Co., Inc. 1965.

West, Cornel. *Race Matters.* Boston, Massachusetts: Beacon Press, 1996.

Williamson, Joel. *A Rage for Order: Black/White Relations in the American South Since Emancipation.* New York: Oxford University Press, 1986.

Winner Chamber of Commerce. *Tripp County, South Dakota, 1909-1984, Diamond Jubilee.* Winner, South Dakota, 1984.

Wintz, Cary D. *Black Culture and the Harlem Renaissance.* Houston, Texas: Rice University Press, 1988.

Woodward, C. Vann. *The Strange Case of Jim Crow.* New York: Oxford University Press, 1955, revised 1957, 1966.

Young, Joseph I. *Oscar Micheaux's Novels: Black Apologies for White Oppression.* Unpublished dissertation. Lincoln, Nebraska: University of Nebraska, 1984.

ARTICLES

Barry, Lee Arlie. "Oscar Micheaux," *Dallas, South Dakota: The End of the Line.* Gregory, South Dakota: Gregory County Historical Society, 1988. pp. 7-8.

Bowser, Pearl and Spence, Louise. "Identity and Betrayal: The Symbol of the Unconquered and Oscar Micheaux's Biographical Legend." *The Birth of Whiteness,* Edited by Daniel Bernardi. New Brunswick, New Jersey: Rutgers University Press, 1996, pp. 56-75.

Carlson, Shirley J. "Black Migration to Pulaski County, Illinois, 1860-1897." *Illinois Historical Journal,* Volume 80, Number 1, 1987. pp. 37-46.

Chambers, Opie. "The Early History of the Rosebud Country," *A Rosebud Review, 1913.* Gregory, South Dakota: Gregory *Times Advocate,* July 1984, reprint of original 1913 publication. pp. 5-7.

Elder, Arlene. "Oscar Micheaux: The Melting Pot on the Plains," *The Old Northwest, A Journal of Regional Life and Letters.* University of Nebraska Press, 1982. pp. 109-125.

Fontenot, Chester, Jr. "Oscar Micheaux, Black Novelist and Film Maker." *Vision and Refuge: Essays on the Literature of the Great Plains.* Edited by Virginia Faulkner with Frederick C. Luebke. Lincoln, Nebraska: University of Nebraska Press, 1982. pp. 109-125.

Gehr, Richard. "One Man Show." *American Film.* May 1991, pp. 35-38.

Green, J. Ronald and Neal, Horace, Jr. "Oscar Micheaux and Racial Slur: A Response to the Rediscovery of Oscar Micheaux." *Journal of Film and Video*. Fall 1988, pp. 66-71.

_____. "Oscar Micheaux's Interrogation of Caricature as Entertainment."

Grossman, James R., "Blowing the Trumpet: *Chicago Defender* and Black Migration During World War I," *Illinois Historical Journal*, Vol. 78; No. 2, 1985, pp. 82-96.

Hebert, Janis. "Oscar Micheaux, A Black Pioneer." *South Dakota Review*. Volume 10, Winter 1973, pp. 63-69.

Hooks, Bell. "Micheaux: Celebrating Blackness." *Black American Literature Forum*. Volume 25, No. 2, Summer 1991. pp. 352-360.

Husaboe, Arthur R. "The Only Black Farmer Between Gregory and Omaha." *An Illustrated History of the Arts in South Dakota*, Arthur R. Husaboe, Editor. Sioux Falls, South Dakota: Center for Western Studies, Augustana College, 1989. pp. 283-284.

Jackson, F.H. "Homesteading on the Rosebud," *A Rosebud Review*, 1913. Gregory, South Dakota: Gregory *Times Advocate*, July 1984, reprint of original 1913 publication. pp. 13-15.

Lewis, Earl. "To Turn as on a Pivot: Writing African Americans into a History of Overlapping Diasporas." *American Historical Review*. June 1995, pp. 765-787.

Narine, Dalton. "Black America's Rich Film History," *Ebony*, February 1988, pp. 132-139.

Peterson, Earl L., Jr. "The Films of Oscar Micheaux: America's First Fabulous Black Filmmaker." *The Crisis*, April 1979, pp. 136-141.

Raines, Edgar F., Jr. "The Ku Klux Klan in Illinois, 1867-1875." *Illinois Historical Journal*, Volume 78, Number 1, 1985, pp. 17-45.

Regester, Charlene. "Oscar Micheaux the Entrepreneur: Financing *The House Behind the Cedars*." *Journal of Film and Video*, #49, 1-2, Spring Summer 1997, pp. 17-27.

_____."'The Symbol of the Unconquered:' Restored by Turner Classic Movies," *Oscar Micheaux Society Newsletter*, Charlene Regester, Editor. Volume 7, Summer, 1998, Durham, North Carolina.

Staff. "The Homesteader," South Dakota High Liner Magazine, July 1996, pp. 19-25.

Strain, David. "Oscar Micheaux, South Dakota's Most Famous Pioneer," *Fifth Annual West River History Conference Papers, September 18, 19, 20, 1997, West River History Conference, Keystone, South Dakota*. Keystone Area Historical Society, Keystone, South Dakota, 1997. pp. 430-438.

Taylor, Clyde. "Crossed Over and Can't Get Back." *Black Film Review*, Vol. 7, No. 4, 1993, pp. 22-27.

Walker, Juliet E.K., "The Promised Land: The *Chicago Defender* and the Black Press in Illinois: 1862-1970." in *The Black Press in the Midwest*, Edited by Henry Lewis Suggs. Westport, Connecticut: The Greenwood Press, 1996.

Woodland, Randal. "Oscar Micheaux." *Dictionary of Literary Biography, Volume 50: African American Writers Before The Harlem Renaissance.* Detroit, Michigan: Gale Research Company, 1986, pp. 208-215.

GOVERNMENT SOURCES

Information on government land sales on the Rosebud Reservation can be found in an Act of Congress dated April 23, 1904, (33 *Stat.*, 254) and an Act of Congress on March 2, 1907 (34 *Stat.*, 1229)

Government correspondence: Council with Rosebud by Inspector James McLaughlin, April 13, McLaughlin to Secretary of Interior, October 5, 1901, Irregular Sized Papers #106, National Archives.

Government correspondence: Assistant Commissioner E.B. Merritt to Mr. Buffalo Bear, April 6, 1922, Indian Central Classified File #211, National Archives.

Government correspondence: Acting Indian Commissioner to Secretary of Interior, April 11, 1970, Letters Received by the Office of Indian Affairs, Second Assistant Commissioner, C.F. Hauke to Superintendent John B. Woods, March 30, 1911, Indian Central Classified File #220, National Archives.

Annual Reports, August 20, 1869, August 29, 1870, Spotted Tail Agency, National Archives, Kansas City; Special Commissioners Edward C. Kimball and Henry E. Alvord to Commissioner of Indian Affairs, June 16, 1873, M234, Roll 252, National Archives; "Background Data on Indians at the Rosebud Reservation", October 1, 1953, Record Group 75, Accession No. 75A457, Box 63085, National Archives, Denver.

Correspondence on the Blair Case: Allotting Agent George C. Crager to Indian Commissioner, November 8, 1893, (#42296) and August 10, 1894, (#30999) in Letters Received by the Office of Indian Affairs, National Archives.

INTERVIEWS

Interviews conducted by the writer at the First and Second Annual Oscar Micheaux Film Festivals, Gregory South Dakota on August 18, 1996, and August 17, 1997, respectively, include the following:

Lee Arlie Barry, Gregory, South Dakota - local historian and Micheaux expert

Pearl Bowser, Independent Scholar and Black Film Expert, New York City

Jack Broome, Principal, Burke High School, Burke, S.D.

Gloria McShann, Grandview, Missouri, formerly of Great Bend, Kansas, friend and neighbor of the Micheaux family in Kansas

Richard Papousek, Gregory County Oscar Micheaux Society, Gregory, South Dakota - ongoing interviews

Charlene Regester, Micheaux Scholar, University of North Carolina

Harley W. Robinson, Jr., Los Angeles, California, second cousin of Oscar Micheaux and long time associate

Interviews conducted by the writer with Herbert T. Hoover, Ph.D., University of South Dakota during the winter of 1996 and spring 1997, and throughout this publication process.

Interview conducted by Steve Plummer, July 27, 1973, with Dick Siler, Rosebud pioneer and Micheaux neighbor, University of South Dakota Oral History Library.

Interviews by the writer with Richard Papousek, Gregory County Oscar Micheaux Society, by telephone, Fall 1998.

Ongoing Interviews by the writer with David Strain, Dakota West Books, Rapid City, South Dakota, summer 1997 and 1998.

OTHER

VIDEO: Bowser, Pearl, et al. *Midnight Ramble.* A Public Broadcasting Corporation video documentary by Northern Lights Productions for *The American Experience*, WGBH, Boston, 1994.

Great Bend Historical Society, Great Bend, Kansas: Memorial Service program for the marking of the grave of Oscar Micheaux, October 8, 1988.

Papousek, Richard. Presentation at Third Annual Oscar Micheaux Festival, August 1998, detailing local "legend" and discussing early local newspaper articles about Oscar Micheaux.

VanEpps-Taylor, Betti C., *Hiding in Plain Sight: The African American Experience in Dakota Territory and South Dakota*, 1802-1970. Unpublished work in progress, 1997-1999.

Archives of the *Chicago Defender*, Chicago, Illinois, 1901-1911, 1919, 1925, 1926.

Archives of the Sioux Falls *Argus Leader*, Sioux Falls, South Dakota, 1948, 1988.

Archives of the Gregory *Times Advocate*, Gregory, South Dakota, 1905-1920, 1996-1998.

New York Sunday Times, New York, New York. September 24, 1995.

Correspondence during 1970-71 between Don G. Coonen, Burke, South Dakota, resident, and Dr. John Milton, Professor of English, University of South Dakota. (John Milton Papers, Center for Western Studies, Augustana College, Sioux Falls, South Dakota and the personal files of Janis Hebert Hausman, Yankton, South Dakota.)

INDEX